George von Trapp

Maria Augusta von Trapp

Agathe von Trapp

Rupert von Trapp

Agathe Trapp

Maria von Trapp

Werner von Trapp

Hedwig Trapp

Lorli Campbell

Johanna von Trapp
Winter

Rosmarie Trapp

Martina T. Dupire

Johannes von Trapp

• Von Trapps on tour in San Francisco in 1946.
front row: **Johanna, Hedwig, Father Wasner, Georg, Maria, Agathe**
back row: **Lorli, Werner, Maria, Johannes, Martina, Rosmarie**

THE WORLD OF THE

VON TRAPP FAMILY

WILLIAM ANDERSON

ACKNOWLEDGMENTS

This book had its origins when my parents took our young family on vacation to the original Trapp Family Lodge. A memorable occasion! In the years since, we have returned many times. As a young journalist, Maria von Trapp graciously granted me an interview, in the bay window of the Lodge. When the re-built Lodge was opened with great fanfare in 1984, I covered the celebration for several magazines. Those articles inspired Japanese writer-translator Yumiko Taniguchi to propose the first version of this book, published by Kyuryudo Art Book Publishing Company of Tokyo. When Johannes von Trapp saw the Japanese edition, he said, "We need this in English." His enthusiasm led to the American publication.

Rupert von Trapp encouraged me early on saying, "Your plan for a factual, historic account of the family and the cultural treasure we were privileged to bring here is to me, very important. I suggest that you interview some of us survivors." I did so, finding Rupert's seven remaining siblings warm and welcoming. Each of them, Agathe, Maria, Werner, Johanna, Rosmarie, Eleonore and Johannes generously shared their memories. Many of their children did the same. The family's rich anecdotes enhance this book from start to finish. Annette Jacobs, Barbara Harris, Hal Peterson and Peter LaManna, former members of the *Trapp Family Singers,* offered fond reminiscences of life on tour. Alix Williamson, the von Trapps' publicist of many years, offered her lively recollections.

Historic photos in this book originated from a variety of sources, including personal collections of the von Trapps. Contemporary photography is the work of Paul Rogers, David Wade, and Molly Peters. Austrian images are courtesy of Stefan Herzl, Zell am See-Kaprun Tourism and Tourismus Salzburg. Thanks to Becky Cassel and the Trapp Family Lodge staff for their input.

Much appreciation is due Cerise Dixon, who is responsible for layout-design work in the current edition of this book. Her creativity, ideas, and editorial skills have resulted in this "museum-in-a-book".

Enjoy this story of the von Trapp family, who have inspired and enriched lives around the world.

— *William Anderson*

Cover and Title page background photo **© Paul Rogers Photography**

Cover photo insert: The von Trapps in 1942. front: Agathe, Werner, Martina, Rosmarie, Maria, Rupert
back: Eleonore, Baron and Baroness von Trapp, Johannes, Johanna, Hedwig

Family Tree page background photo **© Zell am See-Kaprun Tourismus/Faistauer Photography**

TABLE OF CONTENTS

CHAPTER 1   Beginnings ... von Trapps of Austria 8-17

CHAPTER 2   The Captain with Seven Children................................18-29

CHAPTER 3   A Family of Singers 30-39

CHAPTER 4   Salzburg, Austria: Home of the von Trapps.................40-49

CHAPTER 5   Anschluss: The Invasion of Austria 50-57

CHAPTER 6   1938-1939: Between Two Continents.........................58-67

CHAPTER 7   The Trapp Family Singers..68-79

CHAPTER 8   Life At Home 80-89

CHAPTER 9   Settling Down in the Green Mountains 90-99

CHAPTER 10   Wartime Choir and Sing Weeks 100-109

CHAPTER 11   Christmas with the von Trapps 110-121

CHAPTER 12   Post War Years 1945-1947..122-127

CHAPTER 13   On Wings and Wheels 1948-1955 128-143

CHAPTER 14   New Directions for the von Trapps............................144-151

CHAPTER 15   New Songs To Sing: The Sound of Music....................152-163

CHAPTER 16   Loss and Triumph: A New Lodge 164-171

CHAPTER 17   Life at the Lodge...172-181

CHAPTER 18   The von Trapps: A Lasting Legacy 182-187

CHAPTER 19   The Captain's Children ... "We Grew Up!" 188-195

             Chronology...196-197

             Trapp Family Lodge Property Map 198-199

             About the Author...200

THE VON TRAPP FAMILY

Agathe Whitehead von Trapp
(Married in 1911)
1891-1922

Georg von Trapp
1880-1947

Maria Kutschera von Trapp
(Married in 1927)
1905-1987

Rupert
1911-1992

Agathe
1913-2010

Maria
1914-2014

Werner
1915-2007

Hedwig
1917-1972

**Married in 1947
to
Henriette Lajoie**

- George
- Monique
- Elizabeth
- Christopher
- Stephanie
- Francoise

**2nd Marriage to
Janice Tyre**

**Married in 1948
to
Erika Klambauer**

- Barbara
- Martin
- Bernhard
- Elisabeth
- Tobias
- Stefan

Johanna
1919-1994

Married in 1948
to
Ernst F. Winter

Ernst (deceased)
• Johanna
• Florian
• Notburga
• Agathe
• Hemma
• Severin

Martina
1921-1951

Married in 1949
to
Jean Dupire

Notburga
(deceased)

Rosmarie
1929-2022

Eleonore
1931-2021

Married in 1954
to
Hugh D. Campbell

• Elizabeth
• Peggy
• Jeanie
• Polly
• Erika
• Hope
• Martina

Johannes Georg
1939-

Married in 1969
to
Lynne Peterson

• Kristina
• Sam

Chapter 1
Beginnings ...
Von Trapps
of Austria

Austria is one of the world's most beautiful countries. The Alps stretch their peaks heavenward across the length of Austria, with green valleys, pristine lakes, and dense forests between the mountains. Quiet farms dot the glens, with snow-capped mountain ranges as a backdrop.

The Austrians love their land, and they also love their culture. On the Danube River, the capital city of Vienna has often been a haven for artists, musicians, writers, and thinkers. Music has constantly enlivened the Austrians, and their composers have given the world some of its most memorable compositions from the pens of Schubert, Haydn, Brahms, Strauss and Mozart.

Much of the country is Roman Catholic and the festivals, pageantry, and music connected with the church have long been important traditions within the lives of Austrian families. This mixture of faith, celebration, and music-making helped to create the culture of Austria's famous and beloved musical family, the von Trapps.

The saga of the von Trapp family had its origins during the days of the Austro-Hungarian Empire. The Austrian Empire, combined with the Kingdom of Hungary, was ruled by the Habsburgs. The empire consisted of several different nationalities and languages, each retaining its own customs. The land mass included both the towering Alps and seacoast on the Adriatic.

Soon after the formation of the Austro-Hungarian Empire in 1867, August Johann Trapp joined the Austrian Navy. While commanding the SMS *Saida* in the Mediterranean, August Trapp saw his ship safely through a ferocious storm. His bravery and tactical maneuvers came to the attention of Emperor Franz Joseph, who bestowed knighthood upon August von Trapp in 1876. The "von" was added to his name after knighthood; the title hereditary and passed on to his children.

Three children were born to August von Trapp and his wife Hedwig: Hede, Georg, and Werner. The middle child, Georg Johannes, was born on April 4, 1880 at Zara, then the capital of Dalmatia and an Austrian port. (Zara is now known as Zadar, Croatia.) Georg was not destined to know his father well; August von Trapp died in 1884. His wife reared their children on a slender pension as a navy officer's widow.

• **Future parents of the original *Trapp Family Singers*: Captain Georg von Trapp and his wife Agathe.**

• left:
Zell am See, early home of the von Trapps.

© Zell am See-Kaprun Tourismus/ Faistauer Photography

• Captain Georg von Trapp

Korvettenkapitän Georg v. Trapp

Georg's legacy from his father was a passion for the sea. At the age of fourteen he entered the Naval Academy at Fiume on the Adriatic Sea - now Rijeka, Croatia. Intent on becoming an officer in the Austrian Navy, he underwent rigorous training which included social skills, music, dancing and proper etiquette. He was remembered as a fun-loving rascal as well as a gentleman, popular with his comrades.

When he completed training in the Imperial and Royal Austro-Hungarian Navy, Georg and his class embarked on a customary schooner voyage, visiting such places as East Africa, Australia, and Egypt. In the Holy Land Georg acquired seven bottles of Jordan River water, an apt portent for baptizing his first seven children. Adventures continued in 1900 when he participated in a mission to China during the Boxer Rebellion. The Navy dispatched a torpedo boat and three cruisers to protect Austrian interests during an anti-imperialist uprising in northern China. Georg was involved in an Allied expedition which took the fort of Peitang. While there he encountered American troops, developing respect and admiration for them.

Captain von Trapp distinguished himself in maritime studies; his rise in the Imperial Navy was swift. He was transferred from cruisers to battleships, and then to torpedo and destroyer flotillas. He took training in hot air balloons, and became a licensed aviator.

Von Trapp was one of the first to envision the importance of submarine navigation. In 1908 he transferred to the Austrian Navy's submarine division to master the design and workings of torpedoes and submarines. This took him to the Whitehead Torpedo factory in Fiume. Georg von Trapp's professional and personal life was forever impacted by this move.

At a society ball in Fiume in 1909, Captain von Trapp noticed a young woman playing violin. Her gentle spirit and beauty immediately appealed to him. He thought to himself: "She is going to be my wife." The girl was eighteen year old Agathe Whitehead, who lived with her widowed mother and siblings at Villa Whitehead. Agathe's grandfather Robert Whitehead, had invented the torpedo.

At first, a romance between Agathe and the dark-eyed, mustachioed Captain von Trapp was discouraged. There was an eleven-year age span between the two. But Georg became a frequent guest at Villa Whitehead. After a long engagement, Georg and Agathe were married on January 10, 1911, with a festive, formal wedding.

The first home of the von Trapp was a villa at Pola, the seat of the Austrian Navy, on the Adriatic. There the first child was born, a son named Rupert, in November 1911. The second child, a daughter named Agathe, was born in March of 1913. Those were happy times peace for the family. Agathe was capable young wife and mother with a gentle sense of humor and quiet understanding of her husband and his career. Together they created a secure, loving environment for their two children. During his first years of marriage Captain von Trapp commanded the U boat U-6.

World events shook the cozy security of the von Trapps in June 1914. Austria's Archduke Franz Ferdinand, on a visit to Sarajevo, was assassinated by a Serbian nationalist who favored self-rule from Austria. War on Serbia was declared by Austria-Hungary; countries took sides and World War I escalated.

Captain von Trapp was placed in charge of two of Austria's six primitive submarines, first U-5 and then U-14. Under great difficulties he commanded his crews, performing incredible feats. The Captain was a rare commander, making a team of his crew, who were of varied ethnic backgrounds, supporting his men and encouraging them.

Early in the war, all civilians were ordered to leave Pola, so Agathe packed up her children and went to the refuge of her mother's home in the Pinzgau region of Austria, at Zell am See. It was a difficult move, knowing that her husband was in danger, and with the uncertainty as to when she could return to Pola. Agathe's mother was glad to have her family near.

• GEORG and AGATHE
"They seemed to understand each other without words,"
said their daughter Agathe.

OUR EARLY INTRODUCTION TO MUSIC

by Rupert von Trapp

"As far back as my memory can take me, I've always loved music. When I was three years old, my grandmother often played, on the piano, pieces we could sing. She also played waltzes, and I remember her playing chamber music with professional musicians, some of whom became quite well known. She was a gifted amateur, and I guess my sense of musical style began with listening to her play.

My parents both played the violin. I began piano lessons when I was five; my sister Agathe was soon also learning piano and Maria had started both piano and violin. Eventually we began to play sonatas together and some of the easier chamber music of Handel, Haydn, Corelli, and so on.

At the home of relatives, the Auerspergs, at Schloss Goldegg, I remember hearing the great Hungarian pianist Lily Kraus. Also there was the Galimar Quartet (two brothers and two sisters). In those days there was a lot of music everywhere, especially in people's homes.

The Sound of Music movie indicates that my siblings were introduced to music later in our childhood. Our passion for music started at much earlier ages in the Erlhof, our grandmother's lakeside home."

It was for this reason that she designed and built the picturesque country home called "Erlhof" on the lakeshore.

Grandmother Whitehead, whom the little von Trapps called "Gromi", was a dignified matriarch who managed her home with ease and provided a sense of well-being, despite the tragedies of war. Her daughters Agathe, Mary, and Joan knitted for soldiers on the front, played games with the children, sang and made music to help pass the time.

Although Georg came home for furloughs, he was not present when his third child, Maria, was born in 1914. A year later a son was born and named Werner, for his uncle who died during the war.

Daughter Agathe recalled the secure quality of their upbringing and the role of their "Mamá". "Mamá loved her children and her own family. Her youngest sister, our Tante Joan, told me that Mamá actually brought her up and told her useful things for her life ... she knitted snowsuits for us all, as well as woolen caps and mittens. She loved to sew and was very good at it. She made clothes for us and I remember particularly our sailor suits and a bluish-gray coat for me. I can still see Mamá, Tante Mary, and Tante Connie (the widow of Georg's brother Werner) cutting material on the big dining room table. When I was a little older Mamá taught me how to knit and make very small hemstitches."

When we were sick (and we had [al]l the early childhood diseases) [M]amá would care for us personally, [ta]king turns with our nanny."

[Z]ell am See was a haven of quiet [an]d natural beauty, seemingly [tu]cked away from the horrors of [th]e war. Life there revolved on a [re]gular wheel of housekeeping, [fa]mily visits, attending Mass, and [wal]king through the countryside. [To] attend church, or to shop in [tow]n, a short boat ride across the [la]ke was necessary. "Living on [th]e other side of the lake, we were [iso]lated," Maria remembered, [so] we had to become self-sufficient [wi]th our own company."

[O]ne of the earliest experiences [th]e von Trapp children remembered [of] the Erlhof days was family music

• **The Whitehead home, the Erlhof.**

• below: **Zell am See from the Erlhof's side of the lake. "The view is breathtaking ... tremendous."** *-Maria von Trapp*

Photo © Zell am See-Kaprun Tourismus/Faistauer Photography

making. Their mother played piano and violin and sang folk songs with her sisters. Gromi played piano too, sometimes "four-hands style" with her son Frank.

Captain von Trapp's brief respites at home were times to relax from his grueling life in his naval service and to become acquainted with his growing family. But all too soon he was called back to the dismal business of war. His greatest feat for his country occurred in April 1915, when his submarine made an underwater launch at the French battleship *Léon Gambetta*. With a full moon rising eerily over the sea, the Captain and his crew risked their lives to sink the enemy ship and its crew of 600. He later

DODGING A BRITISH DESTROYER

by Georg von Trapp

"One day, at the height of the unrestricted submarine warfare of World War I, on active duty in the combat area, I picked up a British destroyer following me. We zigzagged, maneuvered, did all the tricks known to sailors for throwing off pursuers. Still, that dogged, persistent, infernal destroyer kept on our trail. After four hours we were getting desperate, for if we didn't come up for air soon, we'd die of suffocation. At last I gave the order to come up. I got ready a barrel of oil. When we arose, I had the oil dumped just after we reached top. We took in air, quickly submerged, and when we were in a position to observe again, the destroyer was steaming off — convinced of course that our last emergence was the last throes of a dying ship. Well, when I was again in a position to observe, I noticed that one of my oil valves was leaking enough to send up to the surface a perfect trail which lead the destroyer after us through those terrific four hours' chase."

• **Captain von Trapp**

described the battle as "a kind of duel." Patriot though he was, Captain von Trapp always downplayed his significant leadership role and regretted the loss of life that transpired.

The sinking of the French ship fueled the enemy's fear of what wa[s] perceived as a great Austrian force in undersea navigation. The Mediterranean became an area to avoid.

Captain von Trapp was a nation[al] hero, his name a household word

• **Captain von Trapp was given command of U-5 in April 1915.**

l a headline in the newspapers.
 was given command of a
tured French submarine, the
rie, which had been caught in a
 in Pola. With this new craft he
it on to sink over 60,000 tons of
my shipping.

or his services, Captain von Trapp
 recognized as one of the greatest
oes of the Imperial Navy. He
 awarded the highest national
or, the *Maria Theresian Cross,*
h the rights and privileges and
 of "Baron." The new Baron

von Trapp took his honor modestly;
his daughter Eleonore observed,
"he was always self-effacing,
more concerned about others
than himself."

Life at Erlhof continued at its
slow, idyllic pace, almost as if there
was no war waging. In July 1917,
Georg and Agathe's third daughter
was born and named Hedwig, after
her paternal grandmother.

That same year, 1917, America
entered the war, bringing new
manpower to the struggles. The
Allies — Britain, France, Italy and
now America — formed the Supreme
War Council to plan strategy. A year
later, the war was over. Austria-
Hungary and its allies were defeated.
On November 11, 1918, the armistice
was signed. That same month, the
Habsburg emperor was deposed,
making Austria a republic.

For Agathe and the five von Trapp
children, war's end meant the return
of Papá.

For Captain Georg von Trapp, it
was the end of an era. The Versailles
Treaty stripped Austria of its seacoast; there was no more Austrian
Navy. The Captain described his
feelings, as this chapter of his life
closed: "Slowly and solemnly I
personally raise the flag, wait for
the gun salute, and take her down
again. For the very last time! Tears
stream down every face."

When Captain von Trapp came
home to his family, he was war-
weary and faced with the problem
of finding a permanent home for
his wife and children. His chosen

career over, he wholeheartedly
assumed the position of head of the
family. The rest of his life was spent
as a kindly, understanding patriarch.

For awhile, the reunited family
remained at Erlhof and then lived
nearby at a lake hotel called
"Kitzsteinhorn." It was during
this time in 1919 that their fourth
daughter, Johanna, was born.
Georg and Agathe were beset with
the problems of providing a home
for their large family. Kitzsteinhorn
flooded, making it unlivable.
Austria was plagued by post-war
shortages that affected all levels
of society.

Agathe's brother Robert offered a
solution to the housing dilemma: he
suggested the von Trapps live in a
house he owned at Klosterneuburg,
near Vienna. The property had
been the summer home of Austria's
beloved empress, Maria Theresia,
and was known as *Martinschlossel.*
The family settled into their new
home early in 1921. Not long after,
Georg and Agathe's seventh and
last child was born and named
Martina. It seemed appropriate;
her birthplace stood on the
Martinstrasse close to the
Martinkirche (church). The family
was then complete: Rupert,
Agathe, Maria, Werner, Hedwig,
Johanna, and baby Martina.

Caring for the large family,
the big house, and the broad
surrounding grounds was
accomplished by a staff of maids,
a cook, a governess, and a nurse.
Franz Stiegler, Georg's orderly

• The Captain and Agathe with their first five children.
l-r: Agathe, Hedwig, Werner, Maria, and Rupert. Circa 1919.

from Navy days, also lived on the property with his family. He was a devoted friend of the Captain, and he cared for the farm animals while Gustl, the gardener, oversaw the gardens and orchards — so essential to feed the large household. With food shortages, most Austrians cultivated every available bit of soil.

Agathe von Trapp presided over the entire household of diverse people, ages and needs. She even invited the Captain's widowed sister-in-law and her daughter to join them. Daughter Agathe recalled that her mother "was

beloved by all the servants, and those who survived World War II later remembered her with great affection, saying the best times of their lives was when they were in our service."

The good times at Klosternneuburg did not last long. Scarlet fever invaded the von Trapp nursery, as an epidemic raged all through the area. The children all had cases of varying severity, and Agathe, their mother, eventually contracted the disease.

For weeks, the thirty-one year old mother fought to recover. She

was treated in a Vienna sanitarium for the after-effects of the illness. But her health did not return. On September 2, 1922, the bell in the Martinkirche sounded its solemn toll, marking Agathe von Trapp's death. She was buried in the graveyard outside Klosterneuburg leaving behind her husband and their family of seven children, who were destined to travel far in the world as the Trapp Family Singers.

• Agathe Whitehead von Trapp's legacy to her children included their connection to Zell am See. They all made returns to their family homeplace for the rest of their lives. Maria was 93 when she last returned to the Erlhof in 2008. Once more she was awed by the grand peaks of the Kitzsteinhorn, dubbing it "The Pearl of Austria."

Chapter 2

The Captain with Seven Children

"As long as we were around our father, we were happy."
- Maria von Trapp

above:
back row: **Rupert, Maria, Agathe**
front row: **Johanna, Martina, Hedwig, and Werner**

left:
Salzburg, with the Fortress overlooking Mirabell Gardens.
Photo © Tourismus Salzburg

Before Agathe von Trapp's death, she asked her husband to remarry, in case she did not survive her illness. She sensed that their children, who were accustomed to tender nurturing, would need another motherly influence. At the time of their mother's death, Rupert was nearly eleven, Agathe was nine, Maria was eight, Werner was seven, Hedwig was five, Johanna three, and Martina only eighteen months.

Though the children were motherless, they lived in a web of security. Their governess, Fraulein Freckman, kept the days methodical with lessons, playtime, walks, meals, studying, and regular bedtime. By nature the children were cooperative and self-sufficient; they thrived on routine. Their schoolwork revealed signs of creative talent, and music lessons for the von Trapp children were pleasurable, not tedious.

Georg von Trapp watched lovingly over the lives of his seven children. With his wife gone, his naval career defunct, and the former Austria just a memory, his family became his focus. To further forge his fatherly role he converted from his parents' Lutheran faith to his children's Catholicism.

"We had a beautiful life," said Maria of her childhood. "Our father was very oriented to his children; very fatherly. As long as he was with us he was happy. We were always together. I realize now what an imagination our father had. Every night he told us a story at bedtime. He invented his stories, each one something different. Incredible!"

Utilizing his Navy background, Captain von Trapp participated briefly in a shipping trade business in the North Sea and along the Danube River. When that ceased, he considered other employment, but there was little he was qualified to do as a retired Navy man. The inheritance from Agathe von Trapp sustained the family's needs. Fondly recalling the Marquesas Islands in the South Pacific from his early days in the Navy the Captain dreamed of buying a sailboat and taking his children there. He was already teaching them to be avid sailors. But when the children were not enthused about leaving Austria, the plan was abandoned. It remained in the Captain's mind for years to come.

Next, the Captain thought of moving from Vienna to Salzburg. His older children remembered the beauties of Salzburg well; their mother had taken them there from Zell am See for errands and medical appointments. They knew that Salzburg was one of Austria's most glorious cities ... a place of high mountain peaks, lakes, and the Salzach River. Music seemed to be everywhere; not surprising since composer Wolfgang Amadeus Mozart was born there.

With the children's enthusiasm, their father located a stately villa at 24 Traunstrasse in the quiet suburb of Aigen, a 45 minute walk to the center of Salzburg, or a fifteen minute bus ride. The Captain bought the place in 1923; it was situated in a park-like setting. The gray mansion stood on a shady road at the foot of Gaisberg Mountain. The grounds were wooded and lush, with a barn, a laundry house, and other outbuildings. At the rear of the estate a gate led out to the Aigen railway station where trains stopped en route from Salzburg and beyond. The Aigen Catholic parish church was nearby.

Months of house renovations followed to create a spacious environment for the Captain, his children, and the household helpers. The Captain planned a large garden, and there was also space for cows and chickens.

The von Trapps were settled in their new home in 1925. Entering the front door immediately indicated that this was the home of an Austrian patriot. The Captain's huge red and white Austrian flag from his submarine was prominently hung on the wall.

- **Villa Trapp was originally constructed in 1863. It underwent major renovations when purchased by Captain von Trapp, including adding a third floor. The house went through various residencies and changes after the von Trapp family's occupancy.**

Photo © Reinhard Weidl

Nearby, the massive carved staircase became a magnet for the children — the elaborate railing was perfect for sliding down. The Captain hired a kindly, refined baroness to manage the household. Hans (the butler), a cook, and a laundress were among the helpers employed to fulfill needed tasks. The family's life resumed its routine. The sound of the von Trapps singing and playing instruments resounded through the big house.

There was another sound at Villa Trapp...the Captain's bosun whistle. He used it to communicate with his sailors on submarines. Since the grounds at Villa Trapp were so widespread, he assigned a whistle summons for each of his children. When they heard their signals, they came running. "And we never marched; the whistle was just a way to get our attention. And we wore sailor suits because we loved our father so much," said Agathe.

When the new school term started, Agathe, Maria and Hedwig were enrolled in Salzburg's Ursuline Convent Academy, while Rupert and Werner entered the public school. The children walked to school, a 45 minute trek. Later, bicycles were used. "We had a Daimler car," Rupert recalled, "but most of the time it didn't work." Johanna and Martina had their own governess and were tutored at home.

In 1926 Maria showed signs of exhaustion; doctors believed the eleven year old still suffered from a heart murmur, brought on by the earlier bout with scarlet fever. The long walk to school and back was too strenuous, so the Captain removed her from school to recuperate. Concerned that Maria's studies would suffer, he sought a tutor who could live in and assist his daughter with her lessons. Inquiring at the Nonnberg Abbey in Salzburg, he learned that there was a qualified teacher available. She was 21, a novice at Nonnberg from Vienna: Maria Augusta Kutschera.

• **Maria Kutschera as she looked when she went to Villa Trapp as tutor to young Maria.**

MARIA'S STORY

Maria Augusta Kutschera overcame an early life of hardship. She was born on January 26, 1905 to Karl and Augusta Rainier Kutschera. By the time Maria was two, her young mother died. Her father could not care for his little daughter, so she was taken to live with a kind, elderly cousin. Her circumstances soon changed again. "When I was nine, my other died. I had no near relatives, so the court handed me over to a guardian. This guardian happened to be a passionate Socialist. The Socialists we had at that time were very close to Communists of today. As such, he was a violent anti-Catholic. Suddenly God was out of my life. All the Bible stories I loved in my early childhood were now branded as silly legends. So, although I was baptized, I really grew up outside of the church, hearing nothing but hateful things about it, growing into the same hatred of God and divine things as my surroundings constantly emanated."

The strictness of her guardian, "Uncle Franz," and the lack of warm family life transformed Maria into a youthful cynic. But her environment fostered her strong will and her desire for an education. As a scholarship student, she entered Vienna's State Teachers College for Progressive Education. The pedagogy of the school was liberal and seemed to mirror what

• Maria Augusta Kutschera

• The red-domed Nonnberg Abbey.
Photo © Tourismus Salzburg

was happening in Austria in the aftermath of World War I. Gone were the Habsburgs; Austria was without royals. The war had exhausted Austria, and especially in big cities like Vienna, shortages and hunger abounded.

Young Maria was assisted by *The Society of Friends* (the Quakers). "The famine had gotten so terrible that it was impossible to study or do any work," she said. "In the most crucial moment *The Society of Friends* came to Vienna with food; every student and every schoolchild got one hot meal a day. If it had not been for that one hot meal, I might not have lived."

Something other than food fed Maria's soul: music. Vienna was a grand place to indulge in culture, even in those meager years of the early 1920s. "In Vienna, you really didn't need money to hear good music," she said. "At eight o'clock you go to the Jesuit church to hear a mass by Mozart. At nine o'clock, you walk around another corner to hear a mass by Haydn. At ten o'clock sharp, you go to the Cathedral of St. Stephen's to hear a mass by Palestrina. Then at eleven-thirty you better run. The Imperial Chapel is still in action: the Vienna Philharmonic and the Vienna Choir Boys perform a mass. That's what I did every Sunday — I picked my concerts."

At one of those church services, Maria said she was "thrown off her horse by a special mercy of God." A famous theologian preached so effectively about salvation through Christ that her interest was piqued. At a later encounter with the priest Maria refound her Catholic faith, wholeheartedly so. She was then in her final year of college.

During her student days, Maria became involved with a Catholic youth movement called *Neuland*. The group banded together for outings in the countryside playing volleyball and singing. On hikes through rural Austria authentic folk music was discovered and adopted by the group; in towns and villages euland gave impromtu concerts. ...ese activities, along with a sense ...belonging, appealed to Maria and ...ade a great impact on her. By this ...me she was known as "Gustl." With ...abundance of Marias and Mitzis ...over Austria, her friends simply ...rrowed "Gustl" from her middle ...me: Augusta.

After graduation, Maria was with ...roup on a hiking trip in the ...ps. "I was 8,500 feet up in the ...untains" she said, "standing on ...e edge of a cliff overlooking a ...ole glacier field illuminated by a ...gnificent sunset. I was so over-...elmed by this sight, I thought ...myself that God had given this ...gnificence to me, what could I ...e back to Him? As I thought ...ut it the idea came to me to give ...k all that glorious moment by ...ering a strict convent that would ...rive me of ever seeing it again." ...npetuous and strong-willed ...ever, Maria descended the ...untains and took the train to ...zburg. Asking her way around, ...landed at the Nonnberg Abbey ...trict one she had been told) and ...sented herself as a candidate ...the noviate of the Benedictine ...erhood.

...he had come to the right place. ...ere was so much ecclesiastical ...in Salzburg that it was called ...me of the North." Monasteries, ...eys, churches, and the cathedral ...ed their many bells daily, adding ...he pervasive religious flavor of ...city. Bishop Rupert founded the ...in 696 AD when he arrived as a ...sionary. He originated the

Monastery of St. Peter and the Nonnberg Abbey.

When Maria first ascended the 144 steps leading to the cloistered Nonnberg Abbey, she carried a rucksack, a coil of rope, and ice picks from her mountain climbing adventures. "I have come to stay," Maria announced to the tiny, frail Reverend Mother Abbess, who was unflappable. She accepted the unlikely candidate into the community.

"I was very un-nun-like," Maria said of her unexpected entrance into the cloistered life at Nonnberg. As a graduate teacher, she was assigned to teach in the convent elementary school, a job she relished.

Although Maria sometimes whistled hymns, slid down bannisters, and was overly exuberant, convent life mellowed her. She embraced a belief that became her lifelong motto: that "the only important thing in life is to find out the Will of God and do it."

When Captain von Trapp inquired at Nonnberg about a tutor for his daughter, the nuns decided to send Maria on the temporary assignment. She was astonished when she was told, but understood the Will of God was at work. Maria had no choice.

A dress was hastily found for her. Her few possessions were gathered, including a guitar. Maria Kutschera left the gates of Nonnberg behind and stepped into a new life at Villa Trapp. ~

"SHE WAS FULL OF MUSIC"
by Maria von Trapp, the Captain's daughter

"My first impression of Maria was wonderful when she came to tutor me. She was understanding and caring. She really believed; we thought she was close to God.

Maria had a very free way of teaching me Latin, geography, history and mathematics. She was an outdoor girl; we would go up to the mountains, learning our lessons on the way. Very interesting, unlike my school. She was full of stories, and had a fantastic imagination. When she wasn't teaching me, she helped with the little ones (Hedwig, Johanna and Martina).

When Maria first arrived, she came with a guitar, which she played well. She had a very good alto voice, and belonged to a youth group Neuland. They were against jazz and wanted Austrian music to stay alive. They went through the Alps singing and performing the play "Jederman." Once in a while Neuland members came to visit; we sang with them and they taught us folk dances.

Maria taught us to play practical jokes. Soon after she arrived she hid a live chicken in Rupert's night table. He was stunned. We were not the type of people to do that. She always had to have excitement in her life.

We started singing madrigals with Maria; she taught us to sing in parts. The first song she taught us was 'Tanzen und Springen'. We sang beautifully. I can say that because it's true!"

FINDING THE WILL OF GOD

by Maria von Trapp

*Maria von Trapp was asked to speak to the student body of Brigham Young University in Salt Lake City in 1965. Though she expected a small audience, 9,700 students filled the field house. **The Sound of Music** was at its apex at this time, playing in movie theaters all across America. She explained to students how she transitioned from the Nonnberg Abbey to the von Trapp home.*

• Nonnberg Abbey, Salzburg, Austria

Once upon a time there was a girl who wanted to be a nun. And I tell you, I *really* wanted to be a nun. I handpicked the hardest, strictest, worst-est of all convents I had heard about — an ancient abbey in Salzburg, where I had heard through the grapevine that nuns slept in their coffins. I was very disappointed when I was shown to my bed on my very first evening there.

These good nuns spent a whole year turning a tomboy into a girl, and then spent a second year making a novice out of her. Toward the end of the second year I was called in to see Reverend Mother Abbess. That was a great shock because I was the lowest of the low in the place; the last little postulant, and I just normally didn't see her. I always had a very bad conscience, and for very good reasons. So I took my time to wind my way from where I was, high up there, to where her office was, way down there, thinking all the time: "Just what does she know? This, this, this, or this?"

When I was finally there she said to me, "Maria, I want to know how much you have learned in our house. What is the most important thing in life?" I was so happy that this was all she wanted to know. That I had learned. So, with great conviction I said, "The most important thing in life is to find out what is the Will of God and then go do it."

"Even if it is hard?" she asked. "Even if it is hard," I said light-heartedly. Right then and there I was informed that a navy captain had been there to see her that very morning asking if they could lend him a teacher for his daughter. The nuns had picked me! I was heartbroken. First of all, I didn't want to go. I wanted to stay at the abbey. Secondly, I was a girl from the mountains, and the very little I knew about the navy was from the silent version of the film *Mutiny on the Bounty*.

To make a long story short, I fell in love with the children and married their father; I got used to the father and we were very happy.

• The church steeples and domes in this 1938 color photograph of Salzburg indicate the religious significance of the city.

The von Trapp Wedding Party

• Maria, Johanna, Hedwig, Werner,
a cousin, Rupert, Agathe,
and Martina, who brought
her teddy bears.

Although Maria's designated role was to tutor young Maria, she connected with all seven von Trapp children. Singing was the strongest bond, but she also joined in games, cycled, and brought lively fun into the aristocratic von Trapp home. Maria considered herself "loaned from Nonnberg for ten months", but as the time when she was due to return to the convent approached, the von Trapps did not want her to leave.

Captain von Trapp envisioned Maria as a second wife, and mother for his children. Maria was initially shocked by this proposal ... torn by her affection for the von Trapps and her pledge to serve God in the convent. She hastened back to her only home, the Nonnberg, for counsel.

The Reverend Mother gave the verdict: "We prayed to the Holy Spirit," she explained, "and we found that it is the Will of God that you marry the father and become the second mother to his children." There it was. The Will of God. Maria firmly believed in obeying such a nudge, and stressed this belief in the von Trapp home. She accepted the challenge.

On November 26, 1927, at Nonnberg Abbey, Maria Augusta Kutschera and Georg von Trapp were married. The nuns sang; the seven children were present. And the bride remembered that the wedding was "very, very beautiful."

• **The new Baroness von Trapp.**

chapter 3

A Family of Singers

above:
Maria Kutschera von Trapp

left:
The seven von Trapp children, l-r: Martina, Johanna, Hedwig, Werner, Maria, Agathe, and Rupert. "Our Organ-Pipe photo!" they said.

Maria was 22 when she became the second wife of the Captain, and mother to his children. "I have to do my best in becoming a substitute," she thought at the time. Later she reflected, "At 22, you think nothing of marrying a man with seven children. Georg came with them, almost like a package deal. It took a while for me to mature into him." Captain von Trapp was 47 at the time of his remarriage, twenty-five years his bride's senior.

For Maria, the role of second wife and mother was one she took seriously. She became "Mother" in the family circle, to differentiate from the children's own Mamá. "Mother" read books about second families, trying to avoid any "stepmother" mistakes. She also needed to learn the overseeing of a household, a formidable task for one who had lived in boarding schools and a convent, where meals and housekeeping were not her concern. "The whole thing was overwhelming at first, a household in high-style," Maria remembered. But her husband was patient and helpful — "so very, very kind and understanding," as his wife recalled.

The seven children completely accepted Maria as their second mother. Her lively ways, her outgoing personality, and her curiosity about the world around her commanded their attention. She assisted them with their schoolwork, encouraged their interests, and shared her own passionate loves with her new family. Hiking in the mountains, volleyball, and singing — all carryovers from Maria's *Neuland* experiences — became von Trapp activities.

Of all the influences Maria brought to the children, music remained their favorite pastime. "They were very musical," Maria said. "So I made sure one sang first part, one sang second part, and so on. I sang third part, and it sounded beautiful!" The von Trapps learned a long list of madrigals and folk songs, two hours worth.

Family firesides in the evenings at Villa Trapp were filled with music-making. The Captain played the violin, and instructed Rupert and Maria on accordion. Agathe played guitar and the younger girls studied violin. Of those early music-making experiences, Agathe said, "It was simply part of the climate of our lives. Children of our social standing learned the arts; it was just *done*. You learned music; you learned to draw. In our family we learned what the others did, and the arts were cherished."

- **The nine von Trapp children, including Rosmarie and Lorli.**

Art by Agathe von Trapp.

Besides their music, the von Trapp children discovered other interests to pursue. Rupert decided to become a doctor at the age of ten; Maria thought of missionary work even as a young girl. Agathe's artistic bent was recognized by her father, who arranged for her to study with an Italian watercolor artist. Each of the others — Werner, Hedwig, Johanna and Martina — excelled in artistic pursuits, in addition to singing and playing instruments.

The seven original von Trapp children were destined to become nine. In February of 1929 the Captain and Maria's first child was born: Rosmarie Erentrudis. Two years later, in May of 1931, Eleonore joined the family circle. No longer was eleven year old Martina the youngest. The dark-eyed beautiful baby girls were nicknamed Illi and Lorli. They were now the "little ones" in the nursery. Hedwig, who had a knack for dealing with children, was often in charge of the girls.

The family seemed complete.

Rupert finished his high school education at boarding school in Graz; he then attended the University of Innsbruck. His father wished for a family money manager and encouraged Rupert to major in business. Rupert still held fast to his goal of medicine. Agathe graduated high school in 1931. She then continued more training in foreign languages and art. Werner and Maria studied music at the Mozarteum University in Salzburg. Hedwig, Johanna and Martina still had years left in secondary school. As their second mother said, "It seemed we had a child in every grade in school."

One summer Maria and several of the children attended a music camp. "Early Music" was undergoing a revival — European compositions written between 12? and 1750. The works straddled the Medieval, Renaissance and Baroq periods, and the von Trapps were enamored with the genre. They also were introduced to the tenor soprano, alto and bass recorder, flute-like instruments with a swe clear sound. The recorder was re-introduced in 1919 and was enjoying a new life in music performance. A whole library of music existed for recorder, with works by Purcell, Handel, Vivald Telemann and Bach.

The von Trapps came home excited with what they had learne Little did they know that they would occupy a major role in furthering interest in both Early Music and the recorder.

n the summer months, the
n Trapps' hometown was crowded
th music aficionados who convened
the Salzburg Festival. Since
20, Max Reinhardt's music and
ama festival annually expanded
scope and reputation. The
edieval morality play *Jedermann*
veryman) became a fixture, per-
med open-air on the Cathedral
uare. Other performances included
ozart operas, *Fidelio* (with great
rano Lotte Lehmann), the
nna Philharmonic, and Toscanini
nducting selected operas.
hese attractions helped establish
Festival as a world-class event.
illa Trapp was prime rental
perty during the Festival, so
family often made sojourns to
Adriatic Sea during that time,
ting out their big house to
ebrities and music lovers.
amping, hiking, and sailing
re von Trapp summer activities.
ll the children have learned
mething about sailing a ship,"
org von Trapp said proudly.
he Captain ordered "fold-boats"
de for sailing on the Adriatic.
family visited Pola, the
mer Austrian harbor town,
d camped on the island of
uda. With their experienced
d enthusiastic sailor-father as

teacher, the von Trapp children
expertly maneuvered the fold-boats.

During another summer the
family embarked on a longer sail,
aboard a native cargo vessel called
Archimede. This cruise took them
along the coast of Istria, Dalmatia,
and to the Bocche di Cattaro.

Captain von Trapp was delighted
to be back at sea, showing his family
the phenomenal beauties of the
Mediterranean. Those excursions
rekindled his old desire to supervise
creation of a custom schooner in
which to take his family to the
South Seas. The plans were drawn
up, but world events intervened.

A 1929 headline in an American
newspaper read: "**Wall Street in
Panic as Stocks Crash.**" The resulting
Depression became a world-wide
financial crisis. In Germany, Hitler
and the Nazi Party, on the fringes
for years, gained support as the
economy continued its ruinous

plunge. In 1933 Adolf Hitler
became chancellor of Germany.
Lebensraum, the Nazi concept
for enlarging Germany's land
mass to enhance economic security
and power, was key in creating
"an Empire of Germanic people."
The plan certainly included Nazi
domination of neighboring Austria
— and ultimate world domination.

Captain von Trapp watched
developments in Nazi Germany
with a wary eye.

A serious financial blow was
dealt Austria by Germany during
the 1933 tourism season. Railway
stations in Germany were covered
with suggestive propaganda to
"see Germany first", while avoiding
Austria as a travel destination.
An American travel writer
described the effectiveness of this
tactic: "A fine of one thousand
marks ($250) was imposed by the
German government upon every

• **At the barn behind Villa Trapp
Maria, Agathe, Hedwig and
Johanna impersonate tough
U-boat men, in honor of their
father's heroic exploits at sea.
"We weren't really smoking!,"
Maria said. This photo always
prompted giggles when
Agathe and Maria saw it.**

citizen crossing the Austrian border. How that punished the Salzkammergut! I can still see, only too well, the deserted beaches, the empty inns, the shut up cottages, the long faces of the natives as they waited all summer for the trade that did not come."

The trickle down economic effect reached Austrian banks.

The Lammer Bank of Zell am See, along with its travel agency, were victims of the tourism decline. In desperation, Mrs. Auguste Lammer appealed to Captain von Trapp for aid when her bank was hit by bad debts. To help his friend, the Captain withdrew the family fortune, safely ensconced in a British bank, and deposited it with Lammer Bank. The cash influx was not enough; when the bank failed, the von Trapp money disappeared with it.

"I have no idea how much there was, and how much was left," Rupert said. "My father never talked about that. But something was left, because we stayed in the house." Mrs. Lammer's bankruptcy led her to prison, where she died.

The gracious Villa Trapp became the key to keeping the family afloat. They good-naturedly treated the money loss with a sense of adventure. Maria suggested to her husband that renting rooms would create income. Students, professors, and a social worker became long-term guests. Several of the von Trapp daughters were experts in homemaking skills, so they took over for the now unaffordable household helpers.

The renters filled the house with fresh intellectual, musical and religious life.

A room was converted to a chapel, and daily Mass was held. One morning in 1935 Father Franz Wasner came from Salzburg to say Mass, with the von Trapps singing Gregorian chants and Bach chorales. Franz Wasner was not only a priest, he was a musical genius. After Mass, he joined the family at breakfast, critiquing their singing. This led to regular practice sessions with the informal family choir. Father Wasner introduced them to works of choral music and coached their performance.

Father Wasner liked what he heard of the pure, untrained voices of the seven von Trapps and their stepmother. His coaching sessions became rehearsals as he introduced the group to the works of the sixteenth, seventeenth, and

eighteenth centuries. For the chape they learned motets and masses b Lassus, Vittoria, and Palestrina. Music by Mozart, Haydn, Handel, Isaac, and Thomas Morley followed. Father Wasner was an expert arranger, so he wrote settings for wonderful old folk music and ballads for the singers. "He insisted that we learn everything by heart, so we could concentrate on the music and not on a paper in our hands," said Maria von Trapp.

The von Trapps had two goals: singing to praise God and enjoying their hobby of group singing. There was no notion of going public with their music, though the von Trapps had acquired professional caliber.

The family's vocal mix was perfect for an a cappella choir. Agathe and Johanna were first sopranos; Maria and Martina san

• **The von Trapp recorder ensembl**

• Franz Mathias Wasner became the conductor-composer behind the music of the von Trapp family. He was born December 28, 1905, the son of a farming family from Feldkirchen, in upper Austria. Following his theological studies at the University of Innsbruck he was ordained a Roman Catholic priest in 1929, first serving a parish in Mayrhofen in the Tyrol for a year. He then studied ecclesiastical law in Rome, graduating summa cum laude in 1934. While in Rome he was organist for the Austrian National Church. With his doctorate in canon law completed, he came to Salzburg's Seminarium Majus to teach Gregorian chant. Father Wasner was essential to the von Trapps' career, serving as conductor from their first stage performance to their last, in a musical journey that took them around the world.

ond soprano. The Baroness n Trapp had a lovely mellow) voice. Hedwig also sang alto. ·rner was the tenor, and Rupert bass.

ince much of the music the nily liked was written for early truments, the von Trapps stered the recorder ... those oden, flute-like instruments ·ular in the 1500s and 1600s. ·pera star Lotte Lehmann covered the singing von Trapps ·n she inquired about renting ir home during the Salzburg tival. She heard the family sing l was transfixed. She confronted m saying, "You have gold in r throats!" The opera diva

insisted that they compete at a folk song competition in Salzburg. They agreed. The result: the von Trapp family won first prize in the group singing category.

Lotte Lehmann was delighted. She endorsed the von Trapps wholeheartedly ... "May the Trapp Choir be destined to a successful future. In harmony with the traditions and high expectations of this festival city, Salzburg, it may be anticipated that wherever they go they will reveal, through their singing, the soul of the folk to whom they are so intimately related."

Captain von Trapp was incredulous at Lotte Lehmann's praise.

The idea of his family performing publicly was disquieting; the notion of his wife and children on a stage pained him. He reacted from a parent's protectiveness. Eventually he mellowed and became a supportive backstage father.

1935 ended with a prestigious invitation extended by Austrian Chancellor Kurt von Schuschnigg. The family performed for a formal government affair at Belvedere Palace in Vienna. After they sang, the Captain, Maria and Father Wasner were besieged with suggestions that the family give concerts.

Maria von Trapp was eager to try. In early 1936, Musikverein's small performing hall was engaged

• Lotte Lehmann

• The Aigen parish church, a short walk from the Villa Trapp. There the family did some of their earliest public singing. On Christmas Eve they watched mountain dwellers come down the slopes with lighted, sparkling lanterns, heading to church. The von Trapps incorporated this custom into their own family ritual. The unheated church was frosty; the priests heated the frigid communion wine.

for the von Trapp family's Vienna debut. America's Marian Anderson was singing in the venue's larger hall, so many music critics were present. They also sampled the von Trapp recital. Reviews were glowing: "the singers ... gave evidence of authority and excellent musicianship. The audience was grateful to hear such charming pieces. After intermission the singers appeared in folk costume ... the girls now wore the beloved dirndls and the two men appeared in their Steiermark uniforms, much to the pleasure of the Viennese, who rejoiced and refreshed themselves in the hearty presentation which the singers gave to their mountain calls."

After the triumph in Vienna, "everybody found out we were ripe for the stage," said daughter Maria. "And that developed into our first concert tour."

• The von Trapp family choir, circa 1936; Villa Trapp and the Gaisberg in background.

During the 1937 Salzburg Festival "Kammerchor Trapp" — the Trapp Chamber Choir — performed at the Mozarteum. They were a sensation. "The applause was enormous," noted the Salzburg Chronicle. "They were especially praiseworthy for the joyous spirit with which they sang." The von Trapps created a beguiling onstage appearance. They were attractive young adults, ranging from Martina at age 16 to 25 year old Rupert. Their second mother was only 32. Their colorful Austrian costumes added an aura of gemütlich, so characteristic of Austria. Impresarios from all over Europe offered the von Trapps concert contracts. The family hobby became a budding profession. Singing sessions with Father Wasner became rehearsals. To add variety to their performances the family added an instrumental section of recorder music, along with a viola da gamba played by Werner and a spinet played by Father Wasner. Kammerchor Trapp's repertoire consisted of selections by early masters, madrigals, Austrian folk music and Alpine yodels along with the instrumental music.

In December 1937 the von Trapps made their first concert tour. In Berlin they sang for an audience of 3000 people. In Paris they appeared at the World's Fair. Daughter Maria remembered the exuberant audience. The French applauded, stamped their feet and cheered — demanding twelve encores. The tour included Belgium, Holland, and England. In London, the BBC showcased them on radio and the new broadcasting marvel, television. They sang for Queen Mary at the Austrian Legation. Glowing reviews followed each concert. One critic noted that "Whoever thinks he knows about the heart of Austria and has not heard the Trapp Choir has much to learn." Agathe pasted the press notices into a scrapbook. "They called us the lovely miracle of the von Trapps," she said.

When their tour concluded the members of the von Trapp family were new stars of the concert world. As their stature grew, so did the menacing power of Nazi Germany. ~

• **One of the earliest advertising posters of the "Trapp Chamber Choir."**

HOW I BECAME GEORG VON TRAPP'S TRANSLATOR

by Elizabeth Campbell Peters

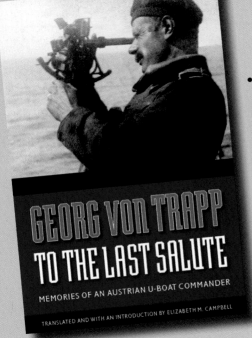

GEORG VON TRAPP
TO THE LAST SALUTE
MEMORIES OF AN AUSTRIAN U-BOAT COMMANDER
TRANSLATED AND WITH AN INTRODUCTION BY ELIZABETH M. CAMPBELL

"I never knew my grandfather, Captain von Trapp. He died in 1947, when his youngest daughter Lorli, my mother, was 16. I grew up hearing my mother and her siblings describing him with superlatives and laughter. I so wished I had been able to know my grandfather personally. I knew that a well-thumbed copy of his 1935 memoir was among my mother's books, and I longed to read it.

It wasn't easy. The title, in thick black Gothic lettering, was 'Bis zum letzen Flaggenschuss.' Translated, this becomes 'To the Last Salute.' Although I spoke German before I could speak English, my fluency with my grandfather's native language was rusty at best. I took German at Middlebury College for two years to learn enough basic grammar and vocabulary to navigate the translation of my grandfather's story of commanding Austrian submarines during World War I.

Life intervened. A teaching career and raising two children slowed the painstaking process of translation until the late 1980s. After a full working day and a workout, I chipped away at the translation for an hour each evening. Finally, I had a first draft. My mother kindly spent a long weekend, figuring out the meanings of archaic colloquialisms in the book. Our work was peppered with her stories of her beloved Papá. We both laughed at his sense of humor, and we admired his tactical skill in leading his submarine crew

through stressful situations. At last, I had a first working draft.

I lived on Martha's Vineyard at this time, so I asked our most famous resident author, David McCullough, to take a look at my manuscript. He graciously read a sample chapter and recommended that I contact his New York publisher, Harcourt Brace.

An editor at Harcourt informed me that people just did not read about World War I; they were only interested in World War II. I tried other publishers, with no luck. Discouraged, I thought of a friend of my mother's family, William Anderson. He had written many books, including the one you hold in your hand: 'The World of the von Trapp Family.'

The timing was impeccable. Bill had previously published a book with The University of Nebraska Press. On the day I called him, a fresh copy of Nebraska's new book catalogue had arrived. He told me this publisher specialized in military history, and my translation might just fit into a niche. The next day, Bill made a cold

call connecting with the right perso[n] at the Press. Bill told me later that [he] pictured the editor on the other end [of] the telephone leaping from his desk so excited to learn of my translatio[n]. A contract arrived. I signed.

During the summer of 2006, I spe[nt] two weekends at the Trapp Family Lodge with my aunts, Agathe and Maria, the eldest daughters of the Captain. We meticulously went through my translation, page by pa[ge], word by word. By the end of our sessions, we had a family-approve[d] manuscript to ship off to The University of Nebraska Press.

Each of the surviving children of Georg von Trapp signed off on the project. They were all thrilled abou[t] the re-publication of their father's memoir. A lovely family publicatio[n] party, hosted by my uncle and aunt Johannes and Lynne von Trapp, was held at the Trapp Family Lodg[e] in March 2007.

Over seven decades after my grand[-]father wrote his book, 'To the Last Salute', it was off and running in [a] beautiful new American edition."

• His children recalled the sounds of a typewriter emanating from the Captain's study as he worked on his memoirs. His celebrity resumed in Austria when the book was published in 1935. He gave many lectures about his submarine commander experience, and appeared on radio interviews.

VON TRAPP TELLS HOW GAMBETTA WAS SUNK

VIENNA, April 30 —

The following details of the sinking of the French cruiser Leon Gambetta have been received from Lieutenant Von Trapp, the commander of the submarine U-5, which sent the cruiser to the bottom.

"A French cruiser, with covered lights, was sighted at midnight 20 miles southeast of Cape Di Leuca. The submarine, from a distance of 500 meters, (about 1600 feet), fired a torpedo at her stern and followed it with a second torpedo amidships. Both hit. From the heeling of the cruiser I concluded that a third torpedo was not necessary".

"Nine minutes after the second shot the ship disappeared. Despite the short interval the French lowered five boats, which are believed to have been saved, as the sea was calm."

"I regret that I was unable to assist in the rescue work."

- left:
  The Captain's first mention in the American press described the Léon Gambetta sinking.

- above:
  Despite accolades for this wartime naval feat, the Captain never was reconciled to the loss of life suffered by Léon Gambetta sailors. The French armored cruiser sank in ten minutes.

Korvettenkapitän Georg v. Trapp

Bis zum
letzten Flaggenschuß

Erinnerungen
eines österreichischen
U-Boots-Kommandanten

Verlag Anton Pustet · Salzburg · Leipzig

Chapter 4

Salzburg, Austria: In the Footsteps of the von Trapps

"When you visit Salzburg, it is like stepping into a fairy tale," said Maria von Trapp of the city where she lived as an aspiring nun, and later as a wife, mother, and singer. Salzburg's magical qualities stem from its magnificent Alpine setting, its rich art and architectural masterpieces, its history and charm. For its many qualities, Salzburg was designated as a UNESCO World Heritage site. It is widely considered one of the most beautiful cities in Europe.

Salzburg has ancient origins. It stands on a Roman settlement named Juvavum, founded in 15 A.D. The substantial salt deposits of the region provided early economic stability, leading to the naming of the Salzach River and the city itself, based on its status as the "Salt Fortress." Barges laden with salt — called "white gold" — plied the Salzach River to distant marketplaces. Salt continued as a major industry for centuries.

When Salzburg fell into near ruin, suffering general decline, the efforts of Bishop Rupert helped to revitalize the city by 696. The Bishop's expansion on early Christian influences already present in Salzburg was significant, including evangelizing among pagans. The city became an important hub of Roman Catholic influence. Prince-Archbishops, under authority of the Pope, ruled Salzburg as an independent principality.

The appearance of the medieval town of Salzburg was transformed with architectural influences of the late Renaissance. Still evident today are magnificent examples of Baroque, Gothic, Romanesque, and Rococo styles. Winding picturesque streets open into broad squares. Salzburg's affinity for early planning, preservation and enhancement of its architectural treasures is considered inspirational.

Salzburg and music are synonymous. As birthplace of composer Wolfgang Amadeus Mozart, Salzburg's musical traditions evolved through the centuries. The annual Mozart Week, celebrated around the composer's January 27th birthday draws international audiences and performers to Salzburg.

Salzburg was the meeting place of Georg von Trapp's family, Maria Augusta Kutschera, and Franz Wasner, their musical conductor-priest. The common bond was music. Together they formed an enduring musical partnership that is now legendary.

• A panorama of the old town of Salzburg is viewed from the Mönchsberg, which was named for the Benedictine monks of St. Peter's Abbey. Other mountains within the municipality of Salzburg include: the Rainberg, Kapuzinerberg, Hellbrunnerberg, and Festungsberg.

• The Getreidegasse is one of the most visited streets of Salzburg's Old City historic district. It is lined with quaint one-of-a-kind businesses. Ornate gilt and wrought iron business signage line the narrow streets, many with pictorial imagery dating from the era when customers could not read. The birthplace of Mozart, Salzburg's most famous son, is nearby.

• The city of Salzburg spreads out from both sides of the Salzach River. The town and river both derive their names from the nearby salt mines. Salt and its export created a major industry for Salzburg, lasting for centuries.

Photos © Tourismus Salzburg

• The Residenzplatz and Fountain is in the heart of the old city sector of Salzburg. The Residenz Palace was the seat of power for prince-archbishops from the 12th century to the early 1800s. The palace was constructed between 1659-1661. The fountain is an example of Baroque design, the world's largest such sample; it was made of marble from the nearby Untersberg mountain.

• From the heights of the Fortress perched above, pedestrians can walk a winding footpath down to Kapitelplatz (the Chapter Square) — or utilize the funicular. The Horse Pond, built in 1732, is on the site of a similar drinking place for horses, used since the Middle Ages.

• The Salzburg Cathedral is at the center of this panoramic expanse of the old city. The current structure was completed in the 17th century with the oldest bells dating back to 1628. In 1944 a single Allied bomb destroyed the Cathedral's central dome. Restoration was completed in 1959. Composer Mozart was baptized here. The Trapp Family Choir sang sacred music within the chapel walls.

Photos © Tourismus Salzburg

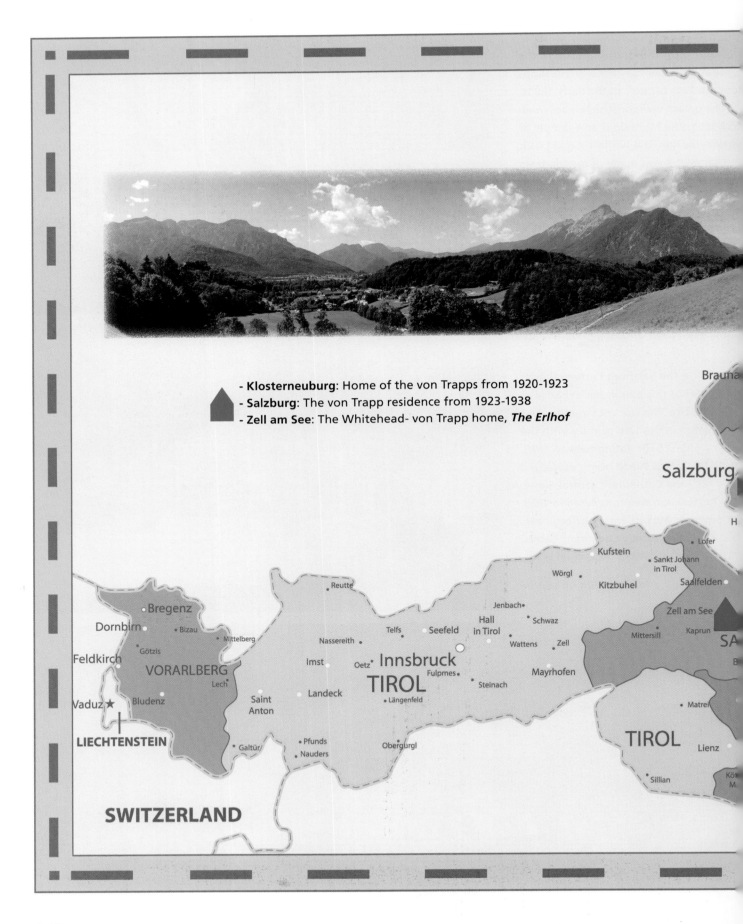

- **Klosterneuburg**: Home of the von Trapps from 1920-1923
- **Salzburg**: The von Trapp residence from 1923-1938
- **Zell am See**: The Whitehead- von Trapp home, *The Erlhof*

• Photo © Tourismus Salzburg   Map image used under license from Shutterstock.com

A Tribute to My Homeland of Austria

by Agathe von Trapp

Austria is a wonderfully beautiful country. It is the heart of Europe; the crossroads from the North to the South, from East to West, and West to East. It has seen the hordes of the Huns, the armies of the Romans, Turks, Napoleon, the Prussians, and the Russians on their quest for world domination.

Austria has assimilated from these different invaders something of their languages, their substance, their cultures ... something for almost every aspect of life. Austria has been robbed and pilfered and yet it survived and stood there on its feet, strong like the mountains, the plains and the lakes that make up its territory. Austria knows how to be rich and how to be poor; how to be proud and how to be humble; how to associate and how to assimilate, and how to cast forth.

Austria knows how to accumulate and how to suffer loss.

It had an exceptional navy and a determined and self-sacrificing army. It always answered the call; it gave what had to be given and it did what had to be done. It is a country of contrasts, of mirth and generosity. It has seen and understood.

Austria had its great men and women. Its composers, musicians and orchestras, its poets, writers, philosophers, scientists and inventors, its doctors, teachers, merchants and businessmen. It has a unique peasant population. It is a colorful country. It dances and sings and sighs and keeps going. "Austria Erit In Orbe Ultima!" It has a sense of the eternal, of never failing in spite of great odds. It fights to the end and rises from its ashes. It is a blessed country.

Austria has its great architects and its humble women, its institutions of learning, its men of great valour. It has its domes, its cathedrals, monuments and museums. Austria has a glorious past and a promising future. It is a country that charms and warms and thrills. It makes you laugh and cry, because for every situation it has a fitting joke. It thrives on its own sense of humor and will not pass up a situation that can be made into a matter of laughter or into a song.

Austria is a queen and will never be anything else.

Wolfgang Amadeus Mozart was born on January 27, 1756, an event his father called "the miracle which God let be born in Salzburg." A musical wunderkind, young Mozart played clavier at age four, and composed his first musical work at five. In his short lifetime (he died in Vienna in 1791) Mozart created an enormous musical output: over 600 compositions including symphonies, choral works, operas, liturgical works, chamber music and concertos.

Like most Salzburgers, the von Trapp family cherished Mozart's prodigious musical legacy. They included the composer's work in their own concert repertoire. Werner von Trapp considered Mozart "the composer who always brings joy to my soul. He always lifts me up." Maria von Trapp affectionately referred to Salzburg's famous composer as "our Mozart."

above:
Mozart's statue, unveiled in 1842, stands in the center of Mozart Square.
Photo ©Tourismus Salzburg

right:
Mozart's birthplace, a museum since 1880.
Image used under license from Shutterstock.com

ANSCHLUSS: the Invasion of Austria

Ve are standing at
he open grave of Austria."
- Georg von Trapp

*was either stay and say
Heil Hitler' or get out."*
- Maria von Trapp

ft:
Mountain climbing with
he Captain in the Dolomite
Mountains of Italy.
ummer of 1938.
r: Johanna, the Captain,
Martina, Werner, Agathe,
nd Hedwig.

Since the Armistice of 1918, which left Austria a defeated land, political and economic conditions in the country were unstable. Many Austrians favored union with Germany, a thought that disturbed the patriotic sensibilities of patriots like Georg von Trapp. Chancellor Dollfuss, who served as Austria's leader from 1932 to 1934 opposed a unified Austria and Germany. He also banned the Austrian Nazi Party. Dollfuss was assassinated as part of a failed government overthrow. His successor, Kurt von Schuschnigg, pledged to defend Austria's status as an independent nation.

The Schuschnigg regime was under continued pressure by Nazi Germany for *Anschluss* — union with Germany. Finally, on March 11, 1938, the inevitable happened. Nazi boots marched into Austria; the country was annexed by Germany.

The von Trapp family sat together, listening to the radio in their library, on the eve of Agathe's twenty-fifth birthday. Suddenly the voice of Chancellor von Schuschnigg was heard. He announced the invasion. German troops were poised to overpower Austria. The Chancellor implored the population not to retaliate, as such an action would only result in great loss of life. The family's shock was interrupted by the tolling of bells pealing from churches in nearby Salzburg. The Captain called police to ask what was happening. He was told that the Nazis had arrived in Salzburg. The bells were "welcoming" the conquerors.

Hitler promptly visited his newly acquired country, with immense crowds, flowers, and flags hailing his presence. On a later visit to Munich, the Captain and Maria happened to observe Hitler and a crowd of guards in a restaurant. They were appalled at the crudeness of the leader of Germany ... and now Austria.

In Salzburg, signs of the German occupation were immediate. The city was festooned with Nazi flags. People mysteriously disappeared; a disabled relative of a von Trapp household helper was never seen again. "We were very much aware of Hitler and what he was doing in Germany," said Maria, who was 22 at the time of the invasion. "My father was horrified. Hitler was full of promises, but already in Germany he had killed Jews and Christians and anybody who challenged his word. He played God. People say they did not know. Impossible. We knew this and we talked about it."

In Salzburg, German soldiers roamed the city. They devoured goods in bakeries and candy shops; they filled restaurants and bierhalls.

Maria von Trapp ignored the order to boycott Jewish shops. While she was in a Jewish-owned business, a Nazi soldier informed her that "You should not be here." Her reply: "Nor should *you* be here in Austria."

Seven year old Eleonore von Trapp (hereafter referred to as Lorli) saw her elementary teachers suddenly replaced by those who were indoctrinated with Nazi beliefs. She was so proud of her father that she had repeated his anti-Nazi feelings at school. Her mother was called in, and warned that Lorli's comments would be reported. When airplanes dropped masses of Nazi propaganda over Salzburg, Villa Trapp was littered with paper. Rosmarie and Lorli helped gather the deluge, knowing how it would upset their father.

In a crowded train station, Lorli was repelled by a multitude of Nazi flags; a virtual forest of red, white, and black banners each with a spider-like swastika. "I so remember the unspoken tension and fright," Lorli said. She loudly voiced her disdain. Out of the crowd a voice warned her: "Be careful. There are ears everywhere."

Every household was expected to fly the Nazi flag. Captain von Trapp told how he avoided the flag edict: "When they sent us a big silk Nazi flag, we refused to hang it out our window. They called me to their headquarters and demanded an explanation. I said, 'I'm sorry, but I don't understand what you want us to hang the flag for.' They told me: to show appreciation that the Führer is coming. I said: All right,

we will decorate if you want, but that color doesn't fit our house well. But we have some very fine Oriental rugs we will hang out th window if you like."

Agathe bicycled into Salzburg; in every public place, on every street, the "Heil Hitler" salute wa heard. It was the day that Hitler made a grand entrance to the plac he now called "My beloved Salzbu His motorcade and subsequent speech drew large crowds.

"A few days later we were asked to sing for Hitler's birthday," the Captain said. "We refused." The family was invited to sing over national radio as a greeting to the Führer from the conquered Austr The implication was transparent: the singing von Trapps, fresh fro high-profile concert tours, would

• "Father Wasner whipped us into a concert-ready group, teaching us polyphonic music, madrigals, chant, and folk songs from many countries, along with instrumentals. We gave concerts as a very small group, as choirs go; there were just nine of us singing."
- Rupert von Trapp

an endorsement for the Nazis. They wanted to use us as a show card," Maria von Trapp said. "We simply said we were not interested," recalled Father Wasner. Then Rupert was approached by the Nazis. As his second mother explained: "To our eldest son Rupert, who was just out of medical college and had barely served his internship, they offered a post as head of one of the great Vienna hospitals. Such a position (with its handsome salary) would have made it possible to support a wife and a home. But we knew that the job they wanted to give to Rupert was really a job taken away from a Jewish doctor." Finally, Captain von Trapp, at 58 years old, was offered a commission in the German navy. His previous wartime feats were remembered. After a twenty-year lapse in active service, the Captain might have been tempted to return to his cherished profession, especially knowing of the great advances in submarines. But serving the Nazis was unthinkable. "I have sworn an oath of loyalty to only one emperor," he said. He declined the Nazi offer.

Maria supported her husband. "If my husband served the Nazis," she said, "it would be a compromise of all the ideals that meant so much to us. There was not an instance of doubt in any of our minds. Exile and persecution would be preferable." No serious reprisals from the von Trapps' non-compliance occurred, except when they attempted to rent concert halls. Venues were mysteriously unavailable.

There was a Nazi in residence at Villa Trapp ... the trusted butler and man-of-all-work, Hans Schweiger. "We loved him," daughter Maria said. "He did everything for us, from serving the meals to cutting the grass to fixing our bicycles." Hans showed the Captain the swastika pinned to his lapel. He implored the family to avoid criticizing the Nazis within his hearing; he was required to report such talk. "Please don't discuss politics at the table," Hans said. "And if you get a chance to go to America, go. *You are on the list.*"

Lotte Lehmann also urged the von Trapps to leave Austria. "They will love you in America," she predicted. Before the Anschluss the diva vowed never to sing for the Nazis. She settled in America, where her fame already preceded her. Fortuitously, Charles Wagner, a New York City concert impresario, heard the von Trapps sing in Salzburg. He offered them an American concert tour for the fall of 1938. This was the family's ticket out of harm's way.

In his diplomatic, fatherly fashion, the Captain gathered his seven older children together to consider the invitation. "My father asked each one of us," Maria said. "If even one of us did not want to go, none of us would go. But everybody wanted to leave. Thank God. Otherwise we would have ended up in the Dachau concentration camp. We couldn't have stayed in Austria any longer."

To seek God's confirmation, the Captain opened the Bible and let a

A TALENT SCOUT REMEMBERS

Agathe von Trapp credited Nelly Walter with discovering the Trapp Family's potential for touring in America. In 1992, Nelly recalled: "It was I who discovered the Trapp Family when I was in Vienna before Hitler marched in. I asked the great Mr. Coppicus from Columbia Concerts (who came regularly to Europe because he was interested in our great stars) to do me a favor and listen to the Trapps. I even took a special hall for this audition. His reaction was, 'How can you imagine I can bring them to New York with that kind of attire?' (The whole family wore Tyrolean peasant outfits). I was very disappointed since the Trapps had come to Vienna at their own expense and money was very tight with them. I quickly asked my good friend Charlie Wagner, who engaged just about everything I presented to him, to do me the great favor to make the trip to Salzburg — which would be very much worth his while. I took a horse carriage to show him all the historical points of Salzburg and drove him up to the Trapp castle. They sang Brahms' Lullaby for Charlie; he was enchanted with the performance and immediately engaged them."

left:
Hedwig (top), Johanna, Agathe, and Martina on a steep hiking climb.

top right:
The von Trapps with their mountain guide, Sepp Mutschlerhner, exploring the Dolomite Mountains.

background:
Peaks of the Dolomites, a range of the northern Italian Alps.

pencil drop on a page. The words from the book of Genesis confirmed his family's leavetaking: *And the Lord said to Abram: leave thy country and thy people, go out of thy Father's house and come into the land which I shall show thee.*

The family felt completely within the Will of God. "God's Will is like a red thread running through our lives," Maria observed, as options unfolded to leave Austria.

In retrospect, Lorli further explained the von Trapp commitment to their faith: "The family, as a whole,

and with the individual's consent, consecrated itself to the Sacred Heart of Jesus. God accepted this consecration and made us His very own special family."

Father Wasner, essential to the choir's existence, received permission from the Archbishop of Salzburg to accompany the von Trapps. As editor of an anti-Nazi Catholic newspaper he was in jeopardy.

A solution for the care and supervision of Villa Trapp emerged. The Captain entrusted the family home to a religious order from the nearby

Borromäum, a Catholic boys' school. The priests were homeless since the Nazis had seized the school property.

Maria von Trapp had her own challenge. She was expecting a child. How would she cope during an uncertain journey from Austria to America, followed by a lengthy concert tour? It was an era when pregnant women remained quietly at home, never appearing on a stage night after night. Maria found a way to conceal the upcoming birth of the tenth von Trapp child. She

• **The family at a guest house in St. Georgen, Italy, where they waited until the appointed time to leave for Amer**

sited a clever dressmaker for
ounsel. "Nothing to it," she was
ld. Costumes were created,
ch fuller above the abdomen
an below. Maria was assured
at the third size would disguise
en twins! In the coming months,
o one guessed Maria's situation.
n early August, prompted by
ans Schweiger's tip that the
ustrian border would soon be
osed, the von Trapps prepared
leave home. They told friends
ey would be hiking in the
ountainous Dolomite region of
Italy, and then going to America
for a concert tour. Although the
von Trapps were Austrian residents,
a technicality made them Italian
citizens. Pola, their former home,
became a part of Italy following
World War I, so the family had
Italian passports. This enabled
them to leave Austria freely.

On the evening before departure,
the family made a pilgrimage to
Maria Plain, where the 1674 era
basilica church overlooked
Salzburg. The church was opened,
candles lit, and the family sang
with deep feeling ... seeking
benediction and consolation.
Outside, in a starlit meadow,
their emotions again overflowed
into song. "It was just to say
goodbye," Martina said. "There
we received our last blessing
in Austria."

Next morning, the Captain
asked daughter Maria to lock
the door to Villa Trapp as the
family left. Each took a suitcase
and rucksack. They boarded a
train at the Aigen station, heading
for Bruneck, Italy and then to
St. Georgen, where they waited
until the voyage to America.
They hiked, climbed mountains
and rehearsed for the upcoming
American concerts.

Captain von Trapp and his
family were among the 130,000
Austrians who left their homeland
in the months following
the Anschluss.

- **Baroness Maria von Trapp
shortly before her family's
flight from Austria.**

INDOMITABLE MARIA

*The von Trapp family gives Maria
great credit for forging ahead with
plans and provisions to escape from
the Nazi regime. Agathe von Trapp
explained her second mother's role
in the process:*

*"Mother had the determination
that helped get us out of Austria.
She was intelligent and she could
organize. She was fun-loving and
was interested in seeing the world.
We did not know anything about
America, so Mother invited some
people to our home who had been
over there, and had written a
book about it. The Lord ordained
Mother to help bring us out of
Austria. He provided the American
concert tour, so that we had a way
out. We dedicated ourselves to the
Lord and He provided."*

The "American Farmer" 7500 tons

PASSENGER LIST

S.S. AMERICAN FARMER

Sailing from

LONDON, FRIDAY, OCTOBER 7th, 1938
TO NEW YORK

Officers:
Commander: Haakon A. Pedersen U.S.N.R.
Executive Officer: Charles K. Gulbe, U.S.N.R.
Chief Engineer : Ellwood Anthony
Purser : Charles Rauth   Surgeon : I. Henry Sachs, M.D.
Chief Steward: Stephen Graves

Adler, Dr. Hans
Anson, Mr. B. Oglie
Anson, Mrs.

Braun, Mr. Wm.
Braun, Mrs. Bertha
Burden, Mrs. Bessie E.
Burden, Miss Roslyn M.

Cargill, Miss Jane
Carr, Miss Margaret J. S.
Cowdrey, Miss Anna B.
Cuttle, Dr. Tracy D.   } Phila-
Cuttle, Mrs.   delphia.
Cuttle, Miss Alexa. E.
Cuttle, Miss Jacquelyn R.

Davoren, Miss Anne
Daw, Mr. Burton
Daw, Mrs.
Donovan, Mrs. Mary
Duff, Mrs. M. N.

Edwards, Mrs. S.

Glaser, Miss V.

Herrington, Mr. F. C.
Holton, Mrs. J. H.
Holton, Miss V. C.
Hoover, Mrs. Lucy
Hope, Miss E. M.
Howard, Mr. Frank G.   Duluth
Hugo, Miss M. L.   minnesota

McCulloch, Mrs. J.
Mallon, Mr. P.   } Cincinnatty
Mallon, Mrs.

Nagel, Mr.

Payne, Mr. Frank
Payne, Mrs.

Peddie, Mrs. Robina
Phelan, Mr. Herbert
Phelan, Mrs. A.
Popton, Mr. Joseph
Powell, Miss Victoria.

Rance, Mrs. Margaret
Reading, Miss Edna
Revy, Mr. R.
Rogers, Miss F. E.
Romney, Mrs. L.
Romney, Miss K.
Romney, Master Richard

Sanders, Mrs. S.
Simmonds, Mr. Albert E.
Simmonds, Mrs.
Stokes, Capt. John H., Jr.
Stokes, Mrs.
Sunde, Mr. T. R.

Tatum, Dr. W. C.
Tatum, Mrs.
Tatum, Miss Debbie J.
Trapp, Mr. George
Trapp, Mrs.
Trapp, Miss Rose Marie
Trapp, Miss Elenor
Trapp, Mr. Rupert   M.D.
Trapp, Mr. Werner
Trapp, Miss Hedwig
Trapp, Miss Martina
Trapp, Miss Agata
Trapp, Miss Maria
Trapp, Miss Joan
Treby, Miss Emily

Ulmer, Mrs. C.

Wahrenbrock, Mr. Howard } Washington
Wahrenbrock, Mrs.
Wasner, Dr. Franz
Weingarten, Miss Rhea
Williams, Mr. S. B.

1938-1939: Between Two Continents

n Europe, the name of Austria
lost. We are trying to show
e Austrian life and customs
e not lost."
- Georg von Trapp

Charles Wagner advanced funds for ship passage to New York City for the eleven von Trapps and Father Wasner. Wagner was an innovator in the American concert business, managing and promoting dozens of attractions. He established hundreds of annual concert series in cities and college campuses across the country. Now he was eager to introduce the von Trapps to the American musical world.

The von Trapps needed ship tickets to America as a requisite to obtaining visas. It was not a favorable time to seek asylum in America. A refugee crisis was underway, prompted by Nazi anti-Semitism and the mistreatment of political dissenters like the von Trapps. American public opinion in 1938 was negative towards European refugees entering the country. Another war seemed inevitable. The lingering Depression was a concern; no one wanted immigrants vying for American jobs. Despite the obstacles, the Captain and his family, along with Father Wasner, received visas.

Early in October the group left their Italian retreat for England. There they boarded the *S.S. American Farmer* for its Southampton to New York City voyage. "We really knew *nothing* about America," said young Maria, "only that there were cowboys, gangsters and skyscrapers. But I think we all inherited something of my father's adventurous spirit of exploration."

The von Trapps checked into the Wellington Hotel in midtown Manhattan, close to Carnegie Hall. The hotel catered to performers and offered rehearsal rooms. "We were the poorest of the poor - refugees", Maria said of those first days when her husband and children reached the safe haven of America. They had four dollars remaining upon arrival, before Charles Wagner advanced funds for living expenses. Aside from Captain von Trapp, no one knew much English. They were unknown as a singing group, had no home, and had no friends in America.

The Americanization of the Austrians began immediately. They discovered Central Park, St. Patrick's Cathedral, museums, elevated trains, subways and department store escalators. They learned the meaning of red and green traffic lights and traffic jams. The family became regulars at the Wellington coffee shop, the Carnegie Deli, and a nearby Chinese restaurant. Rigid economy at each meal was practiced.

The Salzburg Trapp Choir — as the von Trapps were billed on their 1938 tour — first performed at Lafayette College in Easton, Pennsylvania. Father Wasner created a program of Bach, Mozart, Brahms, Schubert, and other early masters to open the concert. Chamber music for recorders,

op left:

he *S.S. American Farmer*
hip carried the von Trapp
amily from England
 America.

ar left:

he *S.S. American Farmer*
assenger list.

ear left:

osmarie and Lorli
n the ship.

spinet, and viola da gamba followed. After intermission, the choir returned to sing folk songs and Austrian yodels. Although no one spoke a word from the stage, "My Old Kentucky Home" was performed in perfect English.

The tour continued through twelve states, with twenty concerts. The family traveled by bus, with a chatty driver offering the Austrians an anecdotal mini-course in American ways. The von Trapps were amazed by the vastness of the country, and the friendliness of the people. The public was fascinated by the singing family, their native costumes, their lives and their flawless performances.

Agathe said that "Audiences sat as if frozen when we started to sing." The sight and sound of her family on the stage had a spellbinding effect on listeners. They were moved by the group's musicality and sincerity.

The von Trapp repertoire of Early Music and folk songs coincided with the increased interest in both genres in music circles and colleges. The music department head at Phillips Academy in Massachusetts wrote Charles Wagner that "the audience was delighted with the Trapp Choir ... the performance of this family is so unique that I hope you will not allow the programme to be cheapened in the slightest degree. Keep this going, and let them realize the highest ideals."

Although Captain von Trapp did not sing on stage, he eased into the role of road manager. His English-speaking skills enabled him to

THE SALZBURG TRAPP CHOIR

Management CHARLES L. WAGNER, INC.
511 FIFTH AVENUE   NEW YORK, N. Y.

• Music critics were generous in their praise of the von Trapps: "When the family completed singing, so taken aback was the audience that a full thirty seconds elapsed before it broke into applause ... then the hall was filled with thunderous acclaim. A novel, refreshing and exquisite program."

andle both radio and newspaper
nterviews. A newspaper reporter
ound him upbeat in discussing the
mily's concert tour, describing him
 "a sturdy, broad-shouldered man,
tired in a gray wide-lapelled
yrolean jacket, who strode briskly
to the hotel lobby, bowed from his
ps with military precision, and
marked: 'von Trapp.'" He discussed
usic readily explaining that "We
ve come over to bring what was
st of the old Austria, its singing
d music." But he was loathe to
ake war predictions or publicly
scuss Europe's troublous situation.
is family sang of peace, joy and
iritual values. In stark contrast,
hile they concertized in Connecticut
November, the Nazi's *Kristallnacht*
upted. The vicious pogroms were
vastating to Jews in Germany
d Austria.

or Maria von Trapp, the concert
p was challenging, with a baby
 the way. As the months progressed,
 wore the largest of her padded
esses to mask her condition.
wspapers described her as buxom,
ple, portly, and finally, stately.
e was ambitious to master
glish, and relied on her husband
fill in the gaps in her vocabulary
en she joined him in interviews.
verything is more delightful in
r country than we anticipated,"
 said. "We have come to bring
 old, the ancient culture to this
utiful country."

When the concert tour concluded,
arles Wagner was stunned to
rn that a tenth von Trapp child
 expected within a month.

• right:
**The Wellington Hotel
on 7th Avenue became
the von Trapps'
"home-away-from-home"
each time they visited New York.**

• left:
**Maria von Trapp in one of
her specially designed dresses.**

below:
**The von Trapps gather before
their Town Hall debut.** front row:
Johanna, Rupert, Agathe; middle:
Maria and Georg; back row: **Maria,
Martina, Werner, and Hedwig.**

THE TOWN HALL

123 WEST 43rd STREET, NEW YORK, N. Y.

STUDENT TICKET Good for Two Seats TOWN HALL Sat. Aftn., Dec. 10 at 3 p.m.

(NO TAX)

STUDENT TICKET

This ticket will entitle bearer to one (or two) Orchestra seat(s) at 25c each, or one (or two) Balcony seat(s) at 15c each for the concert of

THE TRAPP FAMILY CHOIR and YELLA PESSL, Harpsichordist

Town Hall, Sat. aftn., Dec. 10th at 3 p.m.

Present at Town Hall Box Office up to 2:00 P.M. day of concert, or at Steinway Box Office, 113 West 57th Street, up to noon the day of concert.

WILL NOT BE HONORED AFTER 2:00 DAY OF CONCERT

Management: Edith Behrens, 63 West 56th Street, N. Y. C.

Alfred Scott • Publisher • 156 Fifth Avenue, New York

96-12-15A-40

• **The von Trapps on the stage in 1939.**
l-r: **The Captain, Johanna, Agathe, Martina, Maria, Hedwig, Mother, Werner, Rupert, and Father Wasner.**

He canceled upcoming concerts until the baby's arrival. Undaunted the Captain, Maria, and Father Wasner made a strategic career plan: a New York debut of the *Trapp Family Choir* at The Town Hall. The venue, located just off Broadway, had stellar acoustics and a reputation of "not a bad seat in the house." Town Hall was a mecca for introducing new musicians.

A promotional campaign was launched. On December 10, 1938 the *Trapp Family Choir* displayed their talents to an audience of music lovers and curious concert promoters. The *New York Times* reviewed the afternoon concert enthusiastically:

"There was something unusually lovable and appealing about the aggregation as they formed a close semicircle around their self-effacing director for their initial offering, the handsome Mme. von Trapp in simple black, and the youthful sisters garbed in black and white Austrian folk costumes enlivened with red ribbons. It was only natural to expect work of exceeding refinement from them."

Following the Town Hall concert the *Trapp Family Choir* made their first recordings for RCA Victor. There were four extensive recording sessions in RCA's New York studios, concluding just before Christmas.

The family's music and genial personalities won them a circle of American friends and supporters eager to assist them. Their immediate need was housing

• Maria called the day when Johannes was baptized "our first great family feast in America." He thrived on American baby foods, and wore clothes purchased at a Philadelphia department store. His mother predicted that "Johannes promises to be a fine American boy."

below: **Rupert and Johannes, the eldest and youngest of the ten von Trapp children, in 1939.**

iends banded together and found ouse for the von Trapps in the iladelphia suburb of German-wn. Rosmarie and Lorli, who d studied at a convent boarding ool during the hectic weeks the concert tour, now happily oined the family.

On January 17, 1939, during the ourn in Germantown, Johannes org von Trapp was born. It was me of great rejoicing, with other and child healthy, and first American-born von Trapp. her Wasner composed a new g to commemorate the event, e Children's Blessing." It ame a favorite selection during ure concerts.

Vith Europe enveloped in crisis, esounding 72% of Americans onding to a Gallup poll were in favor of accepting larger tas of German exiles. Since the schluss, Austria was considered t of Germany. The United States te Department, along with ngress, was unwilling to open door to increased immigration America. When the von Trapps uested an extension for their s, they were refused. The only ourse was to return to Europe. e Captain arranged for passage the *Normandie*. A series of earances was scheduled for the ndinavian countries. Fifty-six certs transpired during the ng and summer through mark, Norway, and Sweden. ring a respite, Werner and his rs made a stealthy visit to tria. There they collected some

of the family's belongings. Seeing their homeland under Nazi domination cured them of any homesickness. "It was all hypocrisy," Maria declared. "They told people they could go to church, and if they did, they lost their jobs. Children were forbidden to tell their parents what they learned in school. There were shortages everywhere. We had done the right thing by leaving."

The summer of 1939 was a tense one, as Europe hovered on the brink of war. In some places, the von Trapps were suspected of being Hitler's spies.

HEDWIG'S WAR DIARY

Hedwig von Trapp kept a diary during the time her family spent on a Swedish lake during the summer of 1939. These excerpts from her diary entries record the daily activities of the von Trapps, and the German attack on Poland, which signaled the outbreak of World War II.

August 11, 1939
Stalarholmen, Sweden

The night was very good and quiet. At 8 a.m. we had Mass on the porch. This Mass was especially solemn because Father Wasner said it facing us...After communion I forgot to stand up, which is the new way of doing things. Johannes is restless. Mother holds him on her lap. Afterwards we walk to breakfast in the main building. Rosmarie and I climb the cherry tree. One liter is quickly filled. The rehearsal is refreshing and friendly. 12:30 lunch. After lunch I catch up with writing my diary then I took a nap, read and went swimming. Actually every day is the same. I sleep on a blanket while Rosmarie takes my turn of taking care of Johannes. Rosmarie and Lorli are very sweet. They stand on their heads and play leap frog with Johannes. After dinner we sing until 8 p.m. Then evening prayer. The landlord's helper is bringing four kerosene lamps...

September 1, 1939

WAR! Today at 10 a.m. we heard Hitler's speech on the radio from the Metropole Opera in Berlin. There Hitler called an assembly of the Reichstag at 3 a.m., 100 members were absent. Probably in Dachau. Hitler says in his speech he presented Poland with 16 points for negotiation. He wanted to negotiate with a delegation. Poland did not send one.

An English passenger ship which had departed before the declaration of war, was sunk by the Germans...America is outraged because American citizens were on board. There were also refugees on board. England was throwing flyers over Germany to clear up the population about the German government and suggests to topple the government to obtain peace.

September 2, 1939

At 7 a.m. I went to dampen the ironing in the main house. Martha wants to go home to Austria. [Martha was a friend of Maria who accompanied the family on their travels. She came with them to America and waited out the war years.] A taxi was ordered after the mass. Rupert accompanied her to the 9 a.m. steamer to Stockholm. After breakfast, singing mixed with political discussion. I ironed in the main house. Milein (a family nickname for Agathe) is sewing new dresses for Rosmarie and Lorli. Mother is very excited. Every bit of news is listened to. Poland is firing into Breslau. The Germans lost 16 airplanes during the attack into the "corridor." Warsaw radio suggests to the German population to come to reason and shoot at their own government. In Germany listening to foreign radio is forbidden by penalty of death. In the evening Rupert came back with Martha. He dissuaded her from going home. A few of our concerts were canceled in case of mobilization that would occur if England and France declare war. We pray the rosary. Hanni [nickname for Johannes] is very cute and tries to stand up.

September 3, 1939

After breakfast Martha and I went for provisions and shook apples from the tree. Papá took Martha, Agathe and me on a folding boat trip. We started out Papá and Martha in the "Veruda" and Hedwig and Agathe in the "Gombo." [The Captain was able to have the folding boats shipped from Salzburg to Sweden for the family's use.] We sailed towards the east. Behind the bridge the wind decreased, then came from the other direction. We paddled as far as a small island. There we had lunch... from there we sailed to another island. At "home" great excitement. Dr. Wasner and Mother ready to travel. Papá quickly changed and all three went to the 6:30 p.m. steamer — destination Stockholm. Mr. Borjegard, our Swedish manager wants to discuss everything concerning our concerts, which he had arranged in case he is inducted into the army. He fears Sweden might mobilize. After saying rosary we all fall into our beds.

September 4, 1939

Rupert and Werner are going with Maria and Martina on a folding boat excursion. Martha is teaching Rosmarie and Lorli. I clean up the kitchen and watch Johannes. Agathe is finishing the ironing and listens to the news. Mother tells us that a few concerts were cancelled. Borjegard is a stubborn mule. In the afternoon I pasted photos into the "Salzburg Scrapbook", then sang with Mitzi [nickname of sister Maria] and at 4:30 recorder rehearsal. Martina went sailing alone. After dinner we "shouted" folksongs and yodels. Singing and recorder playing is going miserably tonight. The family mood is terrible. Everyone depressed because of concerts we lost and the war news.

KAMMERCHOR ODENSE

STOCKHOLM

die 1000-jährige
moderne
Gross-Stadt

London

KAMMERCHOR
TRAPP

ST KNUD 1086

København

Assens

• The von Trapps' concerts and travels throughout America and Europe in 1938 and 1939 were chronicled in a scrapbook maintained by Rupert, Agathe and Hedwig. Above is a collage highlighting some of the family's itinerary. Keeping scrapbooks of their travels continued throughout their twenty years as a singing, entertaining family.

September 5, 1939

Mass at 8 a.m.

In the night Johannes was very good. He woke up at 6 a.m. and went with me to the beach...he shredded leaves with loud voices. He is getting cuter every day. After mass and breakfast — rehearsal. Then we listened to the news. From the speech one recognized the desperate situation of Germany under the leadership of a madman. Thousands are dying and God gave us a quiet night on the tranquil lake near Stockholm. ~

Whenever they traveled, the von Trapps made new friends, including the Plum family of Denmark. Three weeks into World War II, Captain von Trapp searched for ship passage for the family to return to America, where another concert tour awaited. In this typed letter written in Stockholm on September 22, 1939, Captain von Trapp updates Mr. Plum of the family's current status. His affinity for the English language was a great asset.

My dear friend,

Before leaving Sweden I want to say goodbye and "Auf Wiedersehen" to all our good friends in a moment where nobody knows what might happen to his country and to his folks. We had some concerts here in different places, not as much as we hoped to have, but this terrible war comes in between everybody's plans and also between our concerts. But I must say we had not a bad time, though we longed to be in Denmark again, where we loved it ... you Danish people are much like we Austrians and we felt best with our good friends in Assens and everywhere in Denmark.

I had much trouble to provide tickets for America and now we are so far that we can sail on September 27th on the Bergensfjörd from Oslo. What may we expect in America! We are supposed to stay there until Christmas, but nowadays you can never know what happens and if America should join the war I'm afraid we shall have to stay there and look out how to go on. Besides, our manager over there cut down our concerts to 50%. Our "Schooner" is again far off (the Captain still dreamed of taking the family on a world cruise in a schooner.) But in any case hundreds of our friends in Austria are envying us to be able to stay abroad.

I am at a loss to understand this war. One always has hopes that the English and French will hit a blow, but there is nothing doing. I hope your country will be able to keep out but I am afraid all the neutrals will have to join in the end.

We had so much pleasure to see you all again in Kopenhagen and hope some time we will get good news from you ... we shall write to let you know how we are going on. Our address will be c/o Mr. Charles Wagner, 511 Fifth Avenue, New York City. My wife and children are all right. Johannes just begins to walk and has got four teeth. He is biting apples as long as he does not sleep and we shall have to take a lot of fruit onboard the steamer to let him have enough.

Good luck to you and God bless you all!! Please remember me to Mrs. Plum, your relations, and all our friends in Assens.

Very Cordially Yours,

Georg von Trapp

Despite war conditions the von Trapps returned without incident to America, with six month visas. However, difficulties arose with stringent immigration security. Maria told a *New York Times* reporter that "America is the only place to live; we hope we can become American citizens." Later when immigration officials asked Maria the length of her stay, she rashly blurted out: "I never want to leave!"

Her unwise comment caused the von Trapps to be detained for three grim days at Ellis Island, and classified as "aliens held for special inquiry." Rupert, who fortunately held an immigration visa, frantically worked to get his family free.

Eventually the von Trapps' prominent friends secured their release and they proceeded into New York City. "Mother felt just terrible that she had caused us so much inconvenience," remembered Agathe.

The transplanted von Trapps weathered the storm and took root in a new land, along with twelve million others who passed through Ellis Island during its existence.

The von Trapps and Father Wasner pose for a New York newspaper reporter's camera, after the safe arrival of the SS. Bergensfijörd, which had taken a circuitous route over the Atlantic to avoid possible German U-boat activity.

top row: **Werner and Rupert;**
l-r middle row:
Father Wasner, Johanna, Mother with baby Johannes, Georg, Hedwig, Martina and Maria;
front row: **Agathe, Rosmarie and Lorli.**

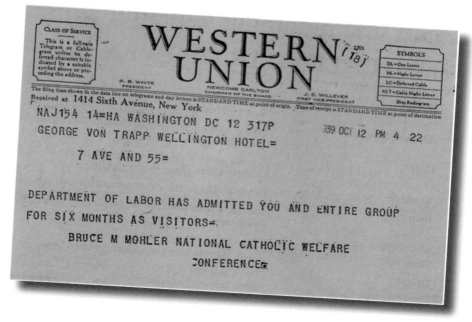

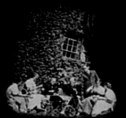

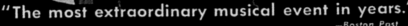

The Trapp Family Singers

As war clouds in Europe intensified the von Trapps felt secure in the haven of America. Their second concert tour, however, was not successful. "Mr. Wagner did nothing to promote us, which was ridiculous," observed Maria von Trapp. "Knowing what publicity means, we didn't know how we could go on, with the halls only a quarter filled. Mr. Wagner was bitterly disappointed in us."

In November 1939 the family sang in Peoria, Illinois to a scant 400 listeners in an 1800 seat venue. Despite low attendance, the newspaper reviewer enthused: "Music as sung by the *Trapp Family Choir* is one of the noblest artistic experiences this side of heaven." A local sponsor, who knew that the 400 who heard the von Trapps would be their best advertisement, booked them again just before Christmas. They packed the house.

The family's future with Wagner's agency was shaky. The Captain, Maria, and Father Wasner enlisted publicist Edith Behrens to promote the group. Their goal was to obtain management by Columbia Concerts, a major New York subsidiary of CBS. The hierarchy at Columbia was unimpressed by the family's Town Hall concerts. Edith Behrens reported: "They say your general mood is too serious, too religious; that you are suited to audiences of real music lovers, primarily Europeans."

Only Columbia's F.C. Schang remained enamored by the singing family. "I would personally have enjoyed working with the Trapp Family," he wrote, "but I have got to be bound by the judgment of my colleagues."

The family's December 1939 tour concluded in Philadelphia. A local music enthusiast, Henry Drinker, offered the von Trapps a house in nearby suburban Merion, opposite his family's home. Gratefully, the von Trapps settled in, with a place to call home in America.

Predictably, Charles Wagner dropped the Trapp Family from his roster of 1940 attractions. Undaunted, Maria requested an audition with Columbia Concerts for her family. Father Wasner rehearsed the choir rigorously. At this crucial audition, they solemnly sang a forty-five minute piece by Bach. Again, Columbia Concerts considered the *Trapp Family Choir* too highbrow for American audiences.

Maria confronted Freddy Schang, asking why her family was rejected. As her son Johannes observed, "My mother was a very, very strong personality. She would walk through walls to achieve her goals." Confronted by Maria's willpower, Schang mellowed. He agreed to gamble on the von Trapps for a year, with one stipulation: he asked Maria to provide a $5,000 advance to promote the group to the concert world. Privately Schang doubted that Maria could raise the cash. But she was dauntless; she borrowed money from supportive friends.

• right:
**Freddy Schang
expertly guided the
Trapp Family Singers
through sixteen seasons
of concerts.**

center:
**"Mother Trapp", Maria,
Johanna, and Martina
in the colorful costumes
worn onstage.**

• below:
**On tour
Father Wasner
insisted on
rehearsals,
especially if he
discovered a
new song
to include in
the program.**

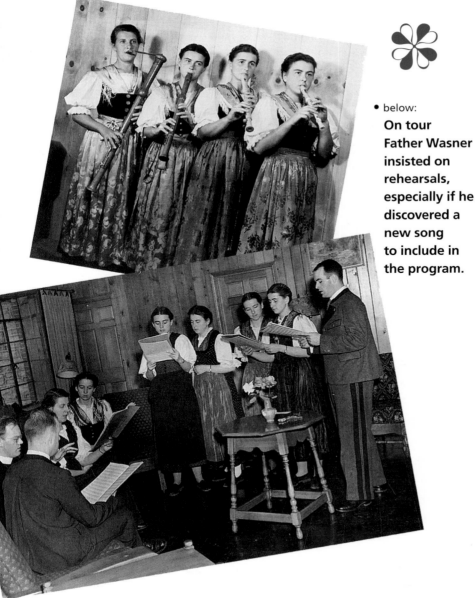

As Hedwig remarked in retrospect, "If it hadn't been for Mother, our concerts would have ended. We would have become cooks and maids in New York."

Freddy Schang, who managed such performers as Caruso, Paul Robeson and Lily Pons, set out to transform the von Trapps' talents into commercial success. He renamed the group ... they became the *Trapp Family Singers*. He coached them on showmanship urging a more informal onstage presence. Father Wasner added American and English folk songs to lighten the classical content of the repertoire.

"They were all top-drawer people Schang declared, "who cooperated 120% with my suggestions."

Sounds of long rehearsal sessions filled the family's loaned house in Merion. Father Wasner was a stern taskmaster as conductor and director. "You have to demand the impossible so the possible can be achieved," he said. Singing sessions of four hours each day were not uncommon when preparing for a new concert tour.

In addition to learning the vocal music, there were recorder rehearsal for the instrumental pieces. Werner practiced his viola da gamba, which was used in combination with recorders and spinet, the latter played by Father Wasner.

Columbia Concerts specialized in the "Community Concert" plan of booking its artists. In this way, towns both small and large could present top-notch entertainment selling subscriptions to a series of concerts. This eliminated individual ticket sales, and introduced musicians like the *Trapp Family Singers* to the blic. Throughout their career, e von Trapps performed for most every Community Concert rganization in America. The rogram had a slogan: *Carnegie all in Every Town*.

The 1940-1941 concert season was e *Trapp Family Singers'* first with olumbia Concerts. On that tour, e singers lost their initial shyness n the stage and their joy in music-aking reached over the footlights their audiences. Previously, as Iaria recalled, "We came on the age, the ten of us, very correct, ry strict. We *never* smiled; for eaven's sake no. We bowed and e sang. If you look down at your idience that grimly, it doesn't ke long until they look back imly — *that* we noticed, and e didn't know why."

They discovered the key to iendly audience rapport in enver. As Maria recalled, while nging with the children onstage, fly was circling my face, so glared at the fly, and the fly uldn't care less. I knew I had take a deep breath, and in went e fly in the wrong throat, and orgot all about being proper; ust coughed and coughed trying get that fly up or down. I finally vallowed it — it was very bitter. was so taken off my composure at I simply stepped forward and id: 'What never happened before s happened now: I swallowed ly.' Everybody laughed, the hole audience and us. That was e turning point. We realized we uld move on the stage, we could iile, we could be at ease, and om then on, it started to be a ccess story."

Freddy Schang was so pleased to hear how the fly broke the ice that he immediately sent a telegram saying, "Your letter of October 29 made me very happy. Congratulations on your diagnosis of American audiences and your adoption of showmanship to bring you *en rapport* with audiences. I really believe you have solved your problem and urge you to expand and continue your explanations."

Maria brought an aura of gemütlichkeit to the concerts. As Agathe said, "Mother had great imagination, and knew how to make things go well on the stage." As her mastery of English evolved, so did her role of stage hostess. She was well suited as commentator — a natural storyteller, with subtle wit and warmth. She welcomed listeners saying, "We feel we have just pushed out one wall of our living room at home and are singing to you as if we were in our own home."

The concerts of the *Trapp Family Singers* made musical history. As the stage curtains parted, a hush fell over the audience, who had never seen a professional singing family. The five girls filed on wearing formal gowns of white silk with black and gold bodices. Their two brothers came on in Austrian-style suits. Their second mother wore a black taffeta gown, and like her daughters, her hair was pulled back plainly with braids coiled in back. Father Wasner conducted the choir in opening selections of sacred music by Bach, Palestrina and Orlando di Lassus. Then Maria introduced her family. "These are my daughters: Agathe, Maria, Hedwig, Johanna, and Martina.

And my sons, Rupert and Werner; our religious leader and conductor, Reverend Franz Wasner. And I am the mother." Captain von Trapp emerged from backstage to make a courtly bow as proud father of the family.

• above:

Backstage before a concert.

below:

"Mother Trapp" … storyteller, singer and group spokesperson.

71

• A map shows the route of the family's first coast-to-coast tour.

• top: **Werner in the driver's seat.**
  center: **Visiting Lotte Lehmann, Santa Barbara**
right: **The family visited the historic Catholic missions on the California coast.**

ht: **Georg and Maria plot out an upcoming concert itinerary.**

center: **"The big blue bus."**
left: **Johannes and the bus driver.**

Introductions were also necessary for the second portion of the program, which consisted of instrumental music. Few Americans were familiar with the ancient recorders, Werner's viola da gamba, or the spinet. Maria explained that the recorder was actually an old-fashioned flute. "My family first started playing the recorder in Austria when we, with Father Wasner, found so much of the older classical music written for it." Then the family demonstrated different combinations of their instruments — a sonata for one or two recorders with viola da gamba and spinet, or a trio of recorders. Works by Vivaldi, Telemann, Couperin, and L'Oiellet were flawlessly rendered. Occasionally instruments accompanied the singing, such as the family's version of Bach's "Jesu, Joy of Man's Desiring."

The instrumental selections were followed by madrigals (a part-song for several voices), particularly of Italian, German, and English composers of the fifteenth and sixteenth centuries. Italian samplings included Orlando di Lassus's "The Soldier's Serenade" and Gastoldi's "Fahren wir froh im Nachen." English madrigals were represented with "Sing We and Chant It," "Now is the Month of Maying," "Sweet Honey-sucking Bees," and "Lady, Your Eye My Love Enforced."

After the madrigals, there was an intermission. The family then changed into their Austrian costumes. The girls wore black dirndls with colorful aprons and scarves and white full-sleeved blouses. The boys wore lederhosen, colorful stockings, and silver-buckled shoes. Audible "oohs and ahs" arose from the audience when the curtains opened to this brilliant array of authentic Austrian attire. This set the scene for a lively selection of Austrian folk songs. There were the lusty hunting songs, rollicking nonsense songs, and romantic folk songs of mountain shepherdesses and their sweethear Then there were yodels; Werner wa a master at this musical form. For t "Echo Yodel," Hedwig disappeared into the wings to provide the appropriate echo effect. "We bring our echo with us," Maria quipped.

The last segment of the concert featured international folk songs. Wherever they traveled the family acquired indigenous music, which Father Wasner arranged and incorporated into their performanc Eventually they sang flawlessly in over a dozen languages, including Latin, Italian, Swedish, Danish, English, Czech, Spanish, Portuguese, French, and a variety of dialects. The concert concluded with encores, which might include Brahms' "Lullaby."

• "We were not a group of soloists. We were all mediocre voices. But under Father Wasner's direction, we became this great sound," said Maria von Trapp of her children. In this outdoor rehearsal photo Father Wasner directs Rupert, Werner, Mother, Hedwig, Johanna, Maria, Agathe, and Martina.

• A reviewer complimented Johanna's singing: "The Kentucky mountain carol 'Jesus, Jesus, Rest Your Head' featured solos in Johanna's clear, ringing soprano." Here she models the costume she and her sisters wore to open concerts.

Critics Chorus

"One of the best ensembles in the world."
— The New York Times

"The most versatile group on the lyric stage."
— Chicago

"No concert can touch the Trapps' concert for that combination of dignity, friendliness, informality, and magnificent music."
— Washington, D.C.

"What this country needs today is to hear more concerts of the mellowness and spiritually colored kind that the Trapp Family gave."
— Roanoke

"Considerably more than 4,000 were in the audience at Masonic Auditorium. The whole occasion, even in so huge a hall, is friendly and informal. It was a true heralding in of the joyous Christmas season by the lark-voiced Austrians."
— Detroit

"A performance by the Trapps is a unique experience. It is an adventure in music mingled with an adventure in personalities."
— Toledo

"Like a mental and spiritual breath from far high places."
— Pasadena

"As refreshing as a summer breeze."
— Baton Rouge

"One of the richest and most beautifully disciplined vocal ensembles this reviewer has been privileged to hear."
— Houston

• left:

The *Trapp Family Singers* became perennial favorites at Jordan Hall in Boston, as seen in this 1941 concert photo.

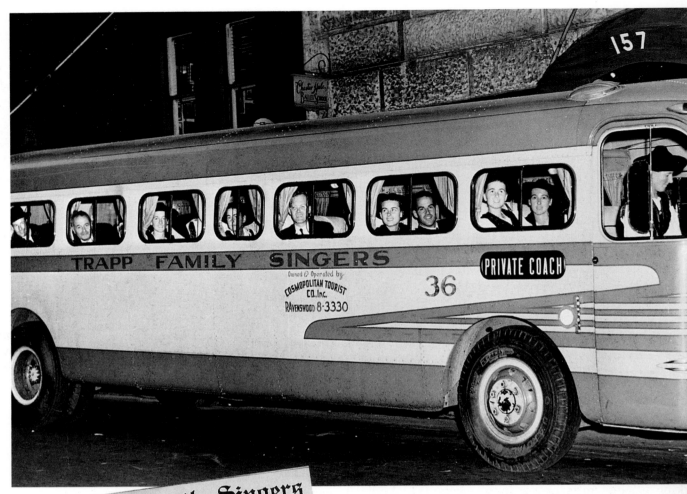

• above:
The bus became a home on wheels for the
von Trapp family when they toured.
By 1941, they had performed coast-to-coast.

right:
After a long day of travel,
Agathe, Maria, Hedwig, and Johanna
wrote letters to sisters Rosmarie and Lorli,
who remained at home so their
schooling would not be interrupted.

Following the performance, people came backstage to visit, or local sponsors held receptions to honor the von Trapps. The hour was sometimes late when the family arrived back at the hotel. Often, an early departure was necessary the following morning to arrive at the next concert town on line. After Mass by Father Wasner, breakfast, and packing, the family was on the road again. They made several tours by car and train, but most often traveled the highways of the United States and Canada in a specially marked bus labeled *Trapp Family Singers*. Concert itineraries were not always geographically consistent; scheduling might require detours and returns, which meant hundreds of extra miles of travel. As much as possible, the bus was made comfortable, and the family passed the long hours reading, rehearsing, chess games, working at handicrafts, or watching the varied landscape of America pass by. After several days on tour, the von Trapps simply became "old troupers"; life on the road was their daily routine. Roadside amenities were sometimes unreliable, so daughter Maria shopped for groceries and prepared lunch in the rear of the bus. "Mitzi's Cafe" fed the family as the bus proceeded to the next concert venue. Long stretches between towns were enlivened by sightseeing. "Mother often arranged sightseeing tours for us," said Agathe. As the family crisscrossed America, they visited historic sites, natural wonders, and beauty spots. "We often wished that every school child could have the opportunity to see all the wonderful places we visited.", said Werner. There were also stops at monasteries and nunneries to sing.

Upon arrival in the next concert town, their routine re-started. There were press and radio interviews, photo sessions, and meetings with local sponsors. Some members of the family checked out the conditions at the concert facility; concert equipment was unloaded and set up; costumes were ironed. Captain von Trapp attended to details as they arose. His children remember how supportive he was in his quiet way, in a life so different from his intended career.

There were also the inevitable pitfalls of constant travel: weather caused delays, forgotten luggage, hotel rooms resold during the concerts. The tours still required a stringent budget. Once, the family assembled in a hotel dining room only to discover the most economical dinner was a dollar. They all rose *en masse* to seek out a more reasonably priced cafe.

Eventually, the *Trapp Family Singers* became Columbia Concerts' greatest group attraction. Their appearances were in high demand; their fee rose to $1,000 per concert. The annual tours expanded from 60 performances to 100, and finally to 125. They experienced more return dates than any other group, and were dubbed "the most heavily booked attraction in concert history."

"Everyone who performs has some stage fright, but we never had very much of it," Rupert observed. "We simply felt people would like what we did, and they did! Singing was fun and I enjoyed it. Some groups complained that their audiences would sit on their hands. We didn't have that problem. We were one of the best small choral groups in existence, ever." Agathe added, "I enjoyed singing with my brothers and sisters because we sounded so

• Maria, called "Mitzi" by her family, was proficient on viola da gamba, the predecessor of the cello and violin. "Though our concert tours were sometimes grueling," she said, "I loved to sing. I belonged to it. I had no choice, really; it was what we were doing. But I always said even if the family had stopped, I would have gone on singing. But of course, I wasn't enough by myself."

good. We were close because we were always singing. We didn't realize how unique our family was. There was not much time for compliments in our family, but I knew Mother was very proud of us. And once my father said, 'Children, you are singing *so beautifully*.'"

Although concertizing was a way to earn a living, members of the *Trapp Family Singers* had a deep sense of mission in their performing. "We knew," said Lorli, "that God had a purpose in our singing, and that is why we kept on; it was that feeling of mission. As soon as we walked on the stage, we could feel a peace descend on the audience, *every time*. God was simply working through us."

Johanna von Trapp

Chapter 8

Life At Home

The family had to stay together survive. They had to be a unit earn a living and make a way the world. The essence of the nily unit was their identity."
- Johannes von Trapp

ee us as a pioneer family d that's the greatest legacy ave from them. My brothers d sisters made a life for mselves by faith and their n hands. Everyone had nething to offer; it was ommunity effort."
- Rosmarie von Trapp

Concert seasons extended from fall to spring, with an interlude during the Christmas holidays. During that time the von Trapps resumed family life at home in Merion, Pennsylvania. Their future as performers was assured; Columbia Concerts offered them 100 concerts for the 1941-1942 season.

"What a privilege it is in America for us to live and speak and think as we please," said Maria von Trapp. Her family was safely ensconced in America, but as "enemy aliens" they were monitored. While absent on tour, the FBI inspected their house in Merion. Nothing of interest was noted excepting a few innocent religious books printed in German.

The family's visas required renewal every six months. In March 1940, Gertrude Ely, a Philadelphia activist, wrote Secretary of Labor Frances Perkins of the von Trapps' visa situation: "I am sending the sheaf of forms made out by Baron von Trapp, making the request that their visitors' visas may be extended. The Trapps have signed a very good contract with the Columbia Broadcasting people ... and a record of the income which they made during the past few months is included in the applications. You remember I spoke to you about getting them renewed. I do hope they may be allowed to stay as they are a very real asset to the country. There are now a few more than thirty days before their present visas terminate."

In 1942 von Trapp family members started the process of becoming American citizens. The Captain did not apply then, but he did offer his naval expertise to the American government. When declined, he was morose; he was willing to do anything he could to defeat the Nazi regime.

The status of Villa Trapp remained a concern. German authorities contacted the Captain, asking to rent the house. They ignored the fact that priests resided there with his permission. The Captain declined the offer. The Nazis consequently confiscated the property and removed the priests. Villa Trapp became a residence for SS leader Heinrich Himmler, occupied when he visited the Salzburg region. Residents of the genteel neighborhood quietly referred to Villa Trapp as "Himmler's flophouse." A formidable high wall was built around the property.

eft:
he von Trapps, circa 1941.
rt by Johanna von Trapp.

top:

Dining at home in Merion was a welcome ritual after hurried meals on tour before evening concerts.

above:

Johanna collects the daily milk delivery.

After the confines of the bus, nightly concerts, and rigors of constant travel, the von Trapps segued into private life at home in Merion. Each member of the family had a role to keep the household of fourteen operating smoothly.

Johanna was the cook; she had been practicing culinary skills since her days in Austria. She was an expert chef, creating American versions of such Austrian specialties as *Leberknodel-Suppe, Wiener Schnitzel mit Gurken Salat, Linzertorte,* and *palatschinken.* Martina assisted by waiting on the table. At each meal the family pronounced the traditional Austrian toast, *"Gesegnete Mahlzeit."* During afternoons they sometimes paused for *"Jause"* — afternoon coffee, along with bread and jam or pastries.

Hedwig was responsible for what she called the "ministry of the laundry" — a formidable task. A creative craftsperson, she also

mastered shoemaking and leather work. Rupert and Werner polishe the family's shoes and did the household shopping. Werner devoted considerable time practicir his viola da gamba, plus tutoring Rosmarie and Lorli on recorder.

Agathe was the seamstress — making clothing and keeping it in repair. The family retained their Austrian outfits, both on stage an off, simply to save money. "Beside Agathe admitted, "we loved our Austrian dresses." The girls said they were never out of fashion — when hemlines went up or down, theirs remained the same. Merion residents were accustomed to seein the von Trapps on streetcars and i stores. They showed friendly intere in the von Trapps' Austrian attire

"We were all very handy," Maria said of her siblings. "We inherited that from our father. Mother had two left hands; she was so impractic She was not a cook. She only kne ow to make apple strudel. Her eat talent was organizing. She as the boss. She handled our ublicity, our concert managers, nd the correspondence. That was big job, to keep our managers orking at Columbia Concerts."

"My father helped everywhere," Maria said. He was a fine carpenter, uilding furniture, including a edroom set for Johannes. Martina ecorated the pieces beautifully ith her paintbrush. "There is othing in the house my husband nnot fix," the Captain's wife told interviewer.

The Captain became the family eacemaker. Rupert admitted that e family's communal lifestyle oked moments of strife. "My usband was very important," said aria. "He sustained us with his uanimity when waves of emotion n high. When the soprano blamed e alto, and the alto blamed the or, then came the father who d: sit down and be quiet."

The Captain's fatherly demeanor othed minor irritations. "Every e of us had something that irked ," daughter Maria explained. here is hardly any family where erything always goes smoothly." ather Wasner's duties as conductor-usician included functioning money manager and spiritual visor. Between tours, he continued earsals. Father Wasner selected w musical compositions for coming tours, and then wrote sh arrangements suited to the nily's voices. He also composed sses, and music to accompany r sixty texts by diverse poets. was, as Maria von Trapp ipped, "Simply music walking und on two legs."

The von Trapps' cooperative family unit was reminiscent of first Christians, working together and sharing, with each receiving what he or she needed. No individual salaries were paid for singing with the *Trapp Family Singers*; especially during the first years, all concert income was required to keep the family afloat.

Despite their success in the concert world, the von Trapps were still refugees. "A refugee is not just someone lacking in money and everything else," wrote Maria von Trapp. "A refugee is vulnerable to the slightest touch: he has lost his country, his friends, his earthly belongings. He is a stranger, sick at heart. He is suspicious; he feels misunderstood ... he is a full-grown tree in the dangerous process of be-ing transplanted, with the chance of possibly not being able to take

• above:
The Captain, busy with a carpentry project.

below:
Father Wasner conducting daily mass in Merion, 1942.

• right:
Werner developed an interest in silversmithing soon after arriving in America.

below:

Martina and an array of her folk art appeared in a 1943 publicity photo.

root in a new soil. As far as we we concerned, our dear Pennsylvania friends took all these feelings awa and made us feel secure."

In Austria the von Trapps were accustomed to a rich world of nati craftsmanship. They found such workmanship becoming extinct in America. "You can't have every-thing ready-made," complained Maria von Trapp. Although she was not skilled at handicrafts, she was proud of her children who were. Between concert tours, the von Trapps pursued those artisan talents.

"My children are very handy anc can do almost anything that can b done with ten fingers," explained Maria. Agathe painted and made exquisite linoleum block prints for a variety of greeting cards. Werner was a silversmith, designing uniqu jewelry. He also wove rugs. Maria fashioned lamps, wooden trays an candlesticks, using a wood lathe. Johanna painted, sculpted, and mastered calligraphy. Martina's folk art was reminiscent of Austri Hedwig turned out tooled leather goods.

A Trapp Family Handicraft Exhibit was held in Philadelphia and New York. Rupert and Moth marketed the family's arts and crafts. Sales helped them through a lean financial period.

For their own amusement, the von Trapp siblings published thei own newspaper. An issue in April 1940 honored the Captain's sixtie birthday. Other editions were fille with caricatures, family humor, and art. Father Wasner, who enjoy outdoor cooking, contributed his recipe for grilled meat and vegetabl which included a cartoon of the

gnified conductor as chef.
e homemade newspapers
culated within the family for
eryone's enjoyment.

uch activities were grist for
ture stories by Alix Williamson,
e family's New York publicist.
relessly she established her clients
musical brand names, which
creased concert bookings. The
app Family Singers, she said,
re the easiest of all musical
minaries to promote. "They were
e holy family' of concerts; the
edia picked up everything I wrote
out them." A singing family
ing and working together during
rtime struck a responsive chord
th the nation. Alix Williamson
o relayed to the media the
unch anti-Nazi sentiments held
the von Trapps, and the reason
their exile from Austria.

s Maria von Trapp explained,
er the mantelpiece at the Merion
use three flags were placed.
ne is the flag of our Austria.
e second is the flag of the schooner
used to sail in the Adriatic. The
rd is Baby Johannes' flag. And it
he Stars and Stripes."

ith photographers in tow,
ix Williamson visited the von
apps at home to gather human
erest stories. "Actually we live
ite normal lives," Hedwig insisted.
erhaps my dress makes this state-
nt sound contradictory, but we
ain our Austrian costumes and
stoms." Those hallmark dresses,
rn on stage and off, were
scribed in Alix Williamson's
blicity releases.

rom her Manhattan office Alix
illiamson secured recording
ntracts, appearances on movie
wsreels, and high profile public

• above:
Hedwig hanging the laundry.

left:
**Rupert was responsible for
the family's shopping.**

below:
**Agathe's artwork was used to
illustrate books and appeared
on greeting cards.**

events for the von Trapps. She successfully booked them on numerous radio shows, including "The United States Steel Hour," "We, the People," and The New York Philharmonic's Sunday afternoon program.

With touring for seven months each year, and busy lives at home, Maria von Trapp was asked what time was left for family life. "But this is family life!" she exclaimed. "We do things together, and that is real family life. That is what is wrong with everybody. They don't *do* things; they buy them at the five & ten store. Everywhere we go, I try to show people how to do things together, which is the way God meant for people to live. We feel very much at home in God's own country."

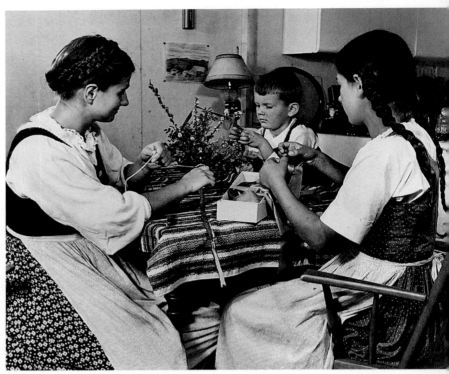

• above:
Johanna, Johannes, and Lorli create Easter decorations using an old Austrian peasant tradition.

below:
Rupert, Werner and Johannes polishing the family's shoes.

far right: **Johanna's painting of edelweiss, her father's favorite Austrian flower.**

Johanna von Trapp '84

• The von Trapps in a pastoral Pennsylvania setting, circa 1941.

Seated at left: **Rupert, Maria, Johannes and Georg.**

Behind them: **Hedwig and Martina**

At right: **Lorli and Agathe**

Back: **Rosmarie, Maria, Johanna and Werner.**

Settling Down in the Green Mountains

he landscape of Vermont is
y consoling; it's always
ere. It's something you can
unt on. Coming from Austria,
rmont was the best place
us to come to. Thank God
having led us to Vermont!"
- Maria von Trapp (Mother)

*very member of my family
covered something
nderful in these mountains
enrich their lives."*
- Johannes von Trapp

ft:
Maria von Trapp on a hike, with
he Green Mountains and the
illage of Stowe in the
ackground.

The von Trapp coat of arms declared: "Nec aspera terrent" (Let nothing difficult frighten you). The von Trapps' first years in America were challenging, but when they concluded their second season with Columbia Concerts, they paid all their debts, leaving $1,000 in reserve. The family decided the time was right to seek out a permanent American home for themselves.

Summers in suburban Philadelphia were often miserably hot and humid, an incentive for the von Trapps to accept an offer from a Mr. Rutledge of Stowe, Vermont. "If you want a summer vacation," he wrote, "I have a place in the mountains you may like." The family rented "The Stowe Away," a roomy tourist home in the cool Green Mountains. The price was right: $100.

The von Trapps were no strangers to Vermont; they had already performed there. On tour, whenever the bus crossed a state line, the driver gave a ceremonial three toots of the horn. He offered a bleak description of Vermont. "All they raise are tombstones. A very unprogressive state." As the family observed the Vermont countryside en route to concerts in Middlebury and Burlington, they were favorably reminded of their Austrian homeland on every side.

"The Stowe Away", where the von Trapps spent the summer, was near Vermont's highest peak, Mount Mansfield. The mountain overlooked a panorama of hills, valleys, forests, and lakes. Nearby was the village of Stowe, first settled in 1794, and one of New England's quaintest towns. During the Civil War Stowe was established as a resort town, known for its natural beauty, peacefulness, and seasonable weather.

"Regardless of what our bus driver thought," Maria von Trapp said, "we loved our vacation in Vermont. We hiked everywhere. When there were no hiking trails, we just pushed through all the underbrush and got scratched all over and enjoyed it all immensely. We climbed Round Top and one of the boys scaled a tree to say, 'The view is gorgeous!' We walked up Mount Mansfield, through Smuggler's Notch, to Bingham Falls, to Moss Glen Falls, and into Stowe Hollow."

• The Luce Hill farm included a horse barn, a cow barn, a house, and outbuildings —
all in disrepair. Maria said, "My husband whispered, 'Look at the house; it is so crooked it doesn't
know which side to fall on.' I replied, 'Georg, we can always build a house,
but we can't build a view.' And so we bought a view!"

"We had begun talking only among ourselves that maybe we should buy a home in Vermont when a very strange thing happened: real estate people began knocking on our door saying, 'We hear you're interested in buying a place in Vermont.'"

Up and down the state of Vermont the family investigated properties, never finding one exactly to their liking. Affordable places were so run down and rickety that they were hardly habitable; better acreages were too costly. As daughter Maria recalled, "Father and Mother drove around Vermont looking for a place to buy. They usually returned saying that places

announced as 'good condition' were in rotten condition. Finally they found a place near a lake, close to Brattleboro, in southern Vermont. They paid $100 as down payment."

As they often did when important decisions confronted them, the von Trapp family prayed, earnestly seeking God's Will for them. For three days and nights, family members took turns praying in a tiny room in "The Stowe Away."

On their last Sunday in Stowe, a friend arrived to tell the family of a farm for sale. "Let's go look," Rupert suggested, and family members agreed to take a drive in the beautiful late summer weather to examine the place.

What the family found was a 660-acre tract of land on Luce H[ill] three miles above Stowe. The plac[e] had magnificent views. The glorio[us] panorama included six mountain[s]. Two-thirds of the farmla[nd] was mountainous and upland past[ure].

"We were in awe at the most beautiful view," daughter Maria said. "We stood on rocks and looked all around — and fell in love with the place. Papa loved it because the horizon was wide — a sunny place! We let the place in Brattleboro go and bought Luce Hill." The von Trapps were now owners of an American home, compliments of a discovery they made: the down payment plan.

Just before the conclusion of their memorable Vermont summer, the family encountered an authentic New Englander. As Maria von Trapp told it, "One day late in August a car stopped at our place and a very quiet gentleman got out. He introduced himself as Mr. Craig Burt of Stowe. And he didn't have so much to say, but I could see he wanted to ask me something. So I finally said, 'Where do you want us to sing, Mr. Burt?'"

He was relieved, for that of course was what he wanted. 'The Army has taken over the CCC camp outside of Stowe, and they asked me to find entertainment for the boys, and so I thought of you people.' (The CCC, or *Civilian Conservation Corps*, was part of President Franklin D. Roosevelt's *New Deal* to provide work projects for young men during the Depression era.) The next Saturday we were picked up in Army jeeps and taken to the CCC camp to sing. Then we agreed to sing a mass for the soldiers the following Sunday."

The von Trapps had been befriended by "The King of Stowe", a nickname that always embarrassed the modest Craig Burt. The kindly, influential man became their "Uncle Craig", a significant link in the family's assimilation process as Vermonters.

• top: **Haying time on the von Trapp family farm, with the Green Mountains in the distance.**

above left: **"Uncle Craig Burt," Stowe lumberman, early promoter of the ski industry, and mentor to the von Trapps.**

above right: **Johannes pitched in to help on the farm even as a young boy.**

• overleaf background: **Stowe's Green Mountains.**
Photo: Paul Rogers Photography

overleaf center: **Stowe and Mount Mansfield when the von Trapp family first knew it.**
Photo: The Vermont Historical Society

The von Trapp land on Luce Hill was fondly called "The Farm." During the 1942-1943 singing tour, a plan emerged among the family. They would create a self-supporting farm home. The first goal was expanding the farmhouse. "We didn't get back to Vermont until late March," Maria recalled. "Snow was still on the ground. We wanted to begin at once to enlarge the house. So we engaged a carpenter and worked alongside him to tear off the roof of the main part of the house. We had the framework up for a second story and new roof when a blizzard struck. We were eating lunch when we heard a terrific crash. 'Oh, they're dynamiting again down in the valley,' someone said. After lunch when I opened the door to the living room I looked right into Vermont. Most of the house was gone! It had fallen right into the cellar."

An Austrian architect living in Stowe designed plans for a twenty-room Tyrolean chalet for the von Trapps. America was heavily involved in World War II at this time; rationing and building restrictions were in force. A new house could not be constructed on Luce Hill, but an addition to the existing one was permitted.

At this juncture, Rupert and Werner were called up for basic training in the U.S. Army. "For a gruesome moment we thought we couldn't sing without our tenor and bass,"

- **March 1943: Family members started renovation of the farmhouse; blizzard winds caused the house to collapse.**

- **An old fashioned crank telephone remained on a wall fragment of the fallen structure. Maria called the Stowe carpenter who assisted with the remodel and asked,"Can you tell me what one does with a fallen down house?"**

Maria recalled. "But there was another Wasner who made different settings for a women's choir and the man's voice: his. America accepted this very naturally."

At home, the brothers were missed sorely. Nonetheless, there was vigorous activity on the Trapp Family Farm, both agriculture and construction. The Captain, Hedwig, and Maria comprised the building crew. The Captain remarked to a visitor: "We could use a few more men on the place." The Vermonter responded, "Yup, or one more of those girls."

Agathe felt invigorated by days digging ditches, mixing cement, planting trees, mowing hay, tending fields and farmyard. The family handled the dairy herd, raised pigs for their own table, or to sell as pork. Maria agreed with her sister, saying, "We were achieving something, building our own home. We loved it." The girls slept in tents or in the hay loft of the barn. Their parents lived in what remained of the old house.

Johannes was four during the first summer on the farm. Of his family's life he said, "We got up early, went to mass, had breakfast, went to work, and worked all day." Mass was held in a chicken coop converted into a chapel.

By mid-summer, the large construction costs ate up the family's financial reserve. Fortunately they were invited to give two outdoor concerts in Washington D.C. Hundreds were turned away at the first performance; thousands were unable to get seats at the second. This enthusiasm proved that seven daughters and their mother could sing without the boys. The concert proceeds paid construction costs on the farm for the remainder of the summer.

Stowe did not immediately warm to the Austrian refugees. "We were *foreigners*," Maria said. "Sometimes people would not even answer our 'Good Morning.'"

• Rosmarie practices the recorder in the remains of the old house. The present Trapp Family Lodge stands on the site of the original farmhouse.

❀ 97

A lifelong Stowe resident recalled the von Trapps "as strangers from a far-off land when they moved here. They wore funny clothes and spoke with accents. Then we went to New York to hear them in Town Hall. It didn't take long for them to fit in here. I think skiing and the von Trapps put Vermont on the map."

A leaking roof was the key to the family's acceptance as Vermonters. Lorli remembered: "We heard that the Stowe High School needed a new roof. They didn't have the money; neither did we. We decided to give a benefit concert just for the Stowe people." Her mother added, "When the concert was over we gave an encore and people applauded like mad. But nobody realized that the concert was over. So we gave another encore. After the fifth encore we said, '*This is it*.' The alderman of the town came up to the stage to shake everyone's hands. Then the whole audience followed suit! We shook 200 hands that night. The school roof was fixed, and we were taken in. That was the turning point. We belonged."

Their own house still remained unfinished. After the concert, the Stowe shop teacher organized a work bee. The roof was shingled. Doors and windows were installed. Tar paper covered exterior walls. The von Trapps witnessed Vermont neighborliness. When they left on tour, the house was ready for winter.

Maria von Trapp observed: "We believed that home could only be in Austria, before we settled in Vermont. Life for the von Trapps took on new meaning."

• top: **Lorli and companions during the house-framing process.**

center: **Mixing cement for the cellar walls.**

bottom: **Stowe rallied for a traditional Vermont work-bee at the Trapps' farm.**

• "We have the most beautiful home I can imagine," said Georg von Trapp when the first version of the house was complete.

left: Up to 144 flower boxes of geraniums bedecked the porches.

below: The bay window was a place to rehearse and visit, with views of mountain ranges.

Chapter 10

Wartime Choir and Music Camp

On December 7, 1941 the *Trapp Family Singers* made their second appearance in Lowell, Massachusetts, presenting a Christmas concert. "The irony of it" reported the local press, "was that while the monster audience listened to an afternoon of peaceful music, and the Baroness pleaded for prayer for her native Austria, Japanese war planes were bombing Pearl Harbor in Hawaii." The ominous news trickled in, and the local concert manager asked Maria to announce the grim event to the packed auditorium. The audience joined the von Trapps singing "My Country 'Tis of Thee". The next day, Congress declared war.

Later in December, Rosmarie and Lorli made their debut at Town Hall, playing recorders. When Rupert and Werner were drafted, both girls were prepared to join the concert group. "I knew I could help fill a gap," Lorli said. "I wasn't asked and never questioned this, because I knew of the sense of mission connected with our singing. I was hustled to New York for voice lessons, and that was that."

• **Lorli and Rosmarie.**

Rupert and Werner entered the U.S. Army's 10th Mountain Division as ski troopers, training at Camp Hale, Colorado. Many of their cohorts were also skiers and outdoorsmen, accustomed to mountainous terrain and arctic temperatures. The von Trapp sons endured rigors of army life, preparing for the difficulties of mountain warfare in Europe. "First we trained endlessly and then we were sent to Texas to stand by for Europe — 14,000 men and 9,000 mules. For the first time in my life I was me. It made no difference to anyone who I was before," Rupert said. He became a medical orderly, since his Austrian degree in medicine was not recognized by the American Army. His colonel frequently consulted him for medical advice.

• **A surprise appearance by Rupert and Werner, on leave from the Army, reunited the singing family. They performed at Hatch Memorial Shell, home of the Boston Pops.**

• **Werner and Rupert.**

While the boys served their country (they received American citizenship when they entered the Army) the rest of the family soldiered on. War imposed restrictions on gasoline use, so tours were made by train. Each day was a challenge, dealing with luggage, finding space on trains filled with the military, and managing for everyone to arrive at the next concert destination on time. In Kansas, a bus to Wichita was canceled, and the local concert manager could produce only a hearse for transportation. The family sang and yodeled all the way, causi[ng] intense curiosity among the peop[le] they passed who had never seen a singing hearse. On arrival in Wichita, people gasped again whe[n] the dirndl-clad von Trapps exited the hearse, alive and well.

At home, Maria's conviction gre[w] that their mountain location was simply too beautiful to keep to themselves. At first there was no way to accommodate everyone wh[o] wished to visit the *Trapp Family Singers* in their home. Then the family learned that the CCC cam[p]

at the foot of their hill was to be demolished. The Army deemed it impossible to heat during winter. Maria's brainstorm in 1944 was to establish a music camp, utilizing the CCC barracks and buildings. The State of Vermont leased the camp to the von Trapps for a period of ten years. As Johannes explained, "My mother had an idea a minute." "We were all for it," his sister Maria said. On tour, audiences were invited to the yet-to-be-established *Trapp Family Music Camp*. A publicity blitz brought hundreds of reservations for ten-day "Sing Weeks" during July and August. When the von Trapps returned to

• top:

An Easter concert at New York's Town Hall in 1945.

above:

A staged publicity shot before a concert in Chicago in 1945 shows the non-singing Captain leading the choir.

- The coverage in LIFE was so significant that Columbia Concerts did a mass mailing to concert managers across America.

- Publicist Alix Williamson persuaded LIFE to feature the von Trapps in 1943. The four page spread depicted their family life on the farm; it also resonated with readers who also had sons in service. LIFE was then the most circulated magazine in America, read by ten per cent of the population. Despite five years of high profile American publicity already, LIFE made the von Trapps a household name. "We became famous overnight," said Johannes.

towe from tour, they had 46 days
 transform the neglected camp
to a charming, comfortable
tting for guests.

Still coping with war rationing,
ey installed plumbing, purchased
rnishings, bedding, dishware and
eded equipment. The barracks
ere painted green; boxes of red
raniums brightened windows.
he barracks were named for famous
mposers: Schubert, Haydn,
ethoven, Mozart, Bach, and
ephen Foster. The airy, screened
ning hall was designated as
ossini Hall. A logical choice; the
mposer of "The Barber of Seville"
is a chef and baker. Johanna von
app was in charge of the kitchen,
nning meals for 120, with the
lp of a kitchen crew.

inal preparations were being
mpleted for the July 10 opening
the camp as the first guests
eamed in. Lorli recalled that
ly father was putting up beds
en a camper walked into her
pty room. My father sent her
k to the office to check in.
hile she was gone, he hastily put
the bed!" Captain von Trapp
pported the camp endeavor fully.
 endeared himself to guests.
'hat a gentle, loving, sweet man,"
mper remarked, "always in the
kground, helping to make the
mp run smoothly for everyone."
he Governor of Vermont
sided over the opening of the

• top:
**The camp in its
mountain setting.**

right:
**Lorli rings
the camp bell.
A camper recalls:
"I attended the
4th Sing Week,
August 15-25, 1949.
I'll always remember
this as one of the
most wonderful
experiences of my life.
It was indeed a
pleasure to know
the Baroness
and her family.
I remember having
a crush on Lorli.
But they were
all fantastic."**

Trapp Family Music Camp. The
first "Sing Week" campers were a
diverse group, ranging in ages from
8 to 80. They included families,
music teachers, professors, students,
retirees, a broker, a bishop, a sales
clerk from Macy's, and an aircraft
factory worker. All races and
religious creeds were welcomed.
After morning chapel and breakfast
Father Wasner conducted choral
singing from 9-11:30. His expertise
as conductor merged many voices
and musical abilities into a beautiful

chorus. During the first session the singers tackled Mozart's "Alleluia" in four parts; next they learned a Bach piece. Father Wasner lectured on the composers and their works. After lunch, afternoons were free for hiking, swimming, or recorder lessons. Pick-up chamber music groups played in Stephen Foster Hall. From 4:30-6, the entire group convened again for singing. Music was everywhere. Maria and several of her sisters taught the recorder lessons. Dedicated players disappeared into the woods to practice. Maria's teaching was so effective that she compiled a method book, *Enjoy Your Recorder.* The book became a standard instruction manual, still available today.

The sounds of dishwashing in the kitchen were accompanied by folk songs. From the chapel came the resonant strains of "Holy God, We Praise Thy Name." The von Trapps sang for their guests in the recreation hall. After supper, there was folk dancing on the lawn, both European style and American. As many as a hundred congregated as Maria explained the steps. Dance music was provided by her husband playing violin, daughter Maria playing the accordion, and other instrumentalists who were pressed into service. As the sun set behind the mountains, campers met for evening vespers in the chapel.

• Right:
A 1944 hand-painted plate by Martina sold in the Music Camp store.

below:
Father Wasner molded a diverse group of voices into a unified chorus during Camp sessions.

• **Camp guests enjoying a lively folk dance directed by Maria.**

"Lights out at 10" was the rule. Maria, often called "Mother Trapp" by camp participants, gave mini-seminars, held storytelling sessions, and led discussion groups. Each member of the family had a role in the camp operation. The hospitality was simple, friendly, and cheery. Excursions beyond the camp were held during the ten day camp session. The group was taken to the top of Mount Mansfield for a picnic and singing. Jaunts to nearby Lake Mansfield and Bingham Falls were planned. A picnic and bonfire near the von Trapp house became a tradition on the final evening together. "We had one hard and fast rule," Maria said. "Nobody could stay at the camp who wasn't actively singing — no onlookers. Since our home was empty because we were all at camp, we put up the non-singing wives, husbands or grandmothers in our house. People liked it so well on our hill that they wanted to come back. And that is how we eventually got into the lodge business."

• above:
Johanna, the Camp's first chief cook, at the farm picnic.

left:
Agathe preparing picnic food.

• **The site of the farm picnic is now the Trapp Family Lodge concert meadow. Lorli is seen at the center of the photo.**

The first season of the *Trapp Family Music Camp* was a success. The camp established itself as a national center for summer music education. Participants returned year after year. Lifelong friendships evolved during the music camps, some of them leading to marriages. Rupert, Martina and Lorli each found spouses through the music camp experience.

"One of my most precious memories happened one August, when camp was over" recalled Agathe. "Guests departed with farewells in word and song, and clean up was in full swing. When the work was done, the family had gone back to our house further up the hill. Maria and I loaded the last odds and ends on a truck and headed home. On the way, a sudden rainstorm poured down. But as we came over the hill where the road dips toward the house, rain turned into a drizzle. To the west the sun was setting and we saw an extraordinary sight! A huge rainbow started in the valley below the house. It extended over a big poplar tree and ended at the porch entrance. The rest of the family stood at the end of the rainbow. We could actually see rainbow colors on their clothes. We joined them on the balcony, with the same rainbow on our clothes. We all stood there, wondering just how this was possible, and what it could mean for us. I thought of Joel 2:30: 'I will show wonders in heaven and on earth.'"

TRAPP FAMILY
MUSIC CAMP
1948

• A copy of the Music Camp 1948 guest roster.

• Under the Trapp Family Music Camp sign.

• Dance time at the Music Camp.

Town Hall 2 SUNDAY AFTERNOONS at 3:00
DEC. 14TH and 21ST

2 Xmas Carol Concerts 2
by the
TRAPP FAMILY SINGERS
DR. F. WASNER, Conductor

Trapp Family Singers
DR. F. WASNER, Conductor

Two Joyous Christmas Concerts

SAT. AFT. **DEC. 18, 1948** AT 5:30
Town Hall
SUN. AFT. **DEC. 19, 1948** AT 3:00
(OVERLEAF)

Chapter 11

Christmas with the von Trapps

*Ve brought our own
ristmas celebration across
e Atlantic Ocean to America."*
— *Maria von Trapp*

*eople left our Christmas
ncerts with a real feeling
holiness. They would come
ckstage and say 'Thank you.
u have just given me my
ristmas.' And we just knew
at God was at work through
r concerts."*
— *Eleonore (Lorli)
von Trapp Campbell*

• **Christmas art throughout
the chapter created
by Agathe von Trapp.**

For the von Trapps, the Christmas season was ushered in when the Captain hung the circular Advent wreath, made of fir twigs, from the living room ceiling. With the lighting of the first of four candles, the

• **The Captain lit the Advent wreath at home in Stowe when
Werner and Rupert were in the military.
On tour, the wreath was hung in the bus. Circa 1944.**

holiday season began. On the same day, each family member drew another's name from a bowl and was responsible for bestowing an anonymous surprise, a treat or good deed each day until Christmas.

The house teemed with preparations, both visible and secretive. In the kitchen, the smells of candy and cookie making filled the air. On the morning of December 6 there was spicy Lebkuchen, marking the visit of St. Nicholas on his feast-day. The kindly saint made his appearance to learn (through letters left by the children) their fondest wishes for Christmas gifts. In Austria, Santa Claus did not leave presents. The Christ Child Himself, assisted by the parents of the house, brought the gifts.

On December 24, the living room was off-limits while the Christmas tree was prepared. It towered to the ceiling, decked with silver chains, candies, ornaments, and real wax candles. When lit, the room was bathed in a warm glow. "Then we read the Gospel of St. Luke, sang 'Silent Night' for the first time at home, and opened the presents," said Rupert. "We all went to bed early, to get some sleep before Midnight Mass. At eleven o'clock, my father would go around singing a certain song to wake us up, as if to the shepherds. It was 'Hirten auf um Mitternacht.'" (*Shepherds Wake Up at Midnight*)

From bedroom door to door, the Captain roused his "shepherds" and each joined him in song, with a lighted lantern. When all were assembled, they walked through the snowy cold to the Aigen parish church, a ten minute trip from

• **The Captain places the star atop the family tree.**

Villa Trapp. The dark night was filled with specks of lantern light as families came down the mountainsides to the village church. In Vermont, the von Trapps assembled in their own home chapel.

The von Trapps brought their Christmas rituals from Austria to America. In time, the customs were transferred to the concert stage.

In 1940 Freddy Schang urged the *Trapp Family Singers* to present Christmas concerts. Father Wasner collected and arranged a potpourri of Christmas music for voice and instruments. The Captain purchased lanterns from Abercrombie & Fitch

for the family to carry onto the darkened stage. Werner suggested sitting around a candle-lit table as the family sang their carols. Lorli asked for a Christmas tree to add gemütlich to the stage.

Concertgoers saw the tall decorated tree, with a long table and chairs nearby. Stage lights dimmed; there was an expectant hush of anticipation. Father Wasner's deep bass began "Hirten auf...". One by one family members joined him, each with lanterns. In the early years, Johannes' lantern barely cleared the floor.

With the glowing tree behind

m, the Trapp Family Singers in the lantern light singing of ristmas. Their repertoire eventually luded an international mix of iday music collected on their rels, including songs from Austria, rmany, Italy, Sweden, England, xico, Spain, and America. Iaria related the folkways of ristmas in her family's homeland, l contributed a song that became trademark. It was *The Virgin's Jaby*. Slowly and meditatively sang in her warm alto voice, h the family humming in background.

he success of the Town Hall iday concerts established that ristmas and the Trapp Family e professionally entwined. It noted that they "provided limpse into an Austria, not torm troopers, but of devout ilies who make music and pay cial devotion to the Christ ild at the season of his birth."

he climax of the concert was *nt Night*. Maria explained Austrian origin, adding that ores would be sung during the cert, leaving *Silent Night* as conclusion. "We have one uest," she said. "As often as you r this song, please say a prayer t our beautiful country, Austria, l rise again." Standing in front

of the lighted tree, the family sang a verse in German, then one in English. The von Trapps hummed the melody as they quietly filed off stage. A tender silence filled Town Hall. One listener remarked, "I never really heard *Silent Night* until I heard the Trapp Family sing it."

First Lady Eleanor Roosevelt echoed the sentiment. When the von Trapps sang at The White House on Christmas Eve 1940, Mrs. Roosevelt mentioned their visit in "My Day", her popular newspaper column. She wrote: "I don't think I ever heard *Silent Night* more beautifully sung."

The overwhelming response to the holiday concerts made them annual traditions in American cities. For sixteen years the weekend before Christmas was reserved for the von Trapps in Town Hall. The family also sang for various charities, radio broadcasts, and early television shows. A "Christmas in New York" movie short featured the family, including the Captain, singing *Silent Night* — one of Austria's most beloved musical exports. The newsreel was seen in movie theaters all over America.

Franz Gruber and Joseph Mohr composed music and lyrics to *Stille Nacht* in Oberndorf, near

• **Stille Nacht, Heilige Nacht.**

Salzburg. It was first heard in Oberndorf's church on Christmas Eve, 1818. Maria von Trapp felt strong kinship with the carol.

Through her mother, Maria was related to the *Rainer Family Singers*, the Austrians who brought *Silent Night* to America in 1840. The song was among the Rainers' repertoire, and it was embraced immediately by American audiences.

Another Christmas song associated with the von Trapps was *Carol of the Drum* composed by Katherine K. Davis in 1941. Father Wasner discovered the song, creating his own arrangement for the von Trapps to sing in concert. They were the first to record the song for Decca Records in 1951. Later, the song title was changed to *The Little Drummer Boy* and became a Christmas standard.

Washington's Constitution Hall was one of the venues that annually booked the von Trapps. During a wartime Christmas, a music critic there explained the mood created by a von Trapp holiday concert: "Love of family, love of music, love of God, and a longing for peace and good will are so powerfully projected in the musical offerings of this family that they transferred their emotion to the audience. At the concert's climax there was hardly a dry eye in the hall."

The von Trapps' fusion of Christmas folkways, beautiful music and family showmanship left their audiences with a profound feeling of peace on earth. ~

• Decca Records issued the family's first long playing Christmas album in 1951. This Christmas classic has remained perennially available since its first release decades ago.

• Town Hall, circa 1950. l-r: **Lorli, Agathe, Maria, Werner, Father Wasner, Johannes, Martina, Hedwig, Mother.**

Father Wasner's compendium of both rare and familiar Christmas music was published in 1950. The book was illustrated by Agathe von Trapp.

• below:
Family members promoted and signed *The Trapp Family Book of Christmas Songs* when it was newly released. l-r: Maria, Martina, Johannes, Agathe, Mother, and Father Wasner.

Von Trapps on Tour
DECEMBER 20, 1946

Excerpt from a feature story "Salzburg in the Subway"

Looking as if they had just stepped off a Tyrolean Alp, Baron Georg von Trapp, Baroness Maria von Trapp, their seven daughters, two sons, and Dr. Franz Wasner arrived in their own bus. After morning mass delivered by Father Wasner, the family split up for the morning. The Baroness attended to bookings; Rosmarie, Lorli, and Johannes studied with a French-Canadian tutor. The older girls shopped at handicraft stores for materials for presents that each Trapp makes for every other Trapp. Baron von Trapp bought supplies for the 20 room house he and his family built on a 660 acre farm in Vermont. When we got to their hotel at noon, the bright-eyed Trapps had been up for hours. In one small room we found Rosmarie, Johanna, Hedwig and Agathe all dressed alike, and at work on various handmade gifts. Silver and gold tinsel angels were strewn across the bed. Agathe's linoleum blocks for Christmas cards were piled on a table. Hedwig was smocking a blue cotton nightdress for her mother. On the floor sat Johannes, wearing a green-trimmed suit exactly like his father's and brother's, knitting a length of blue rope into bedroom slippers for his mother. In the next room Werner was forging handmade silver medallions and chains. Rupert was expected late that evening from the University of Vermont where he is in his last year of medical school.

"Please come in and don't get scared of the mess! I know it's terrible," said Hedwig, sweeping a partly finished hand-fringed scarf off a chair.

"Gosh darn it," Johannes mumbled, as he nearly dropped a stitch.

"Johannes!" reproached his sisters in unison.

• Lorli and her father prepare the lanterns for the family procession on stage.

• **Seventeen year old Rosmarie and seven year old Johannes pass time with a backstage chess game. Johannes played a corder duet with Johanna during the concert.**

above right:
Two Marias. Maria assists Mother with coiffure.

right:
The dressing room in Town Hall: Johanna, Lorli, Mother, Maria and Martina.

All photos taken at Town Hall on December 21, 1946)

"I wish I could have Werner's blow torch. I was going to melt the tinsel down and make something of it. We're very busy now. It's close to Christmas and we don't have much time in New York for school," Johannes said, his Yankee twang contrasting sharply with his sisters' soft German accents.

Johannes (quite confident in his first press interview) said he was anxious to leave New York and get on to his favorite stop of every concert tour: Texas. "I like Texas best," he said, "because it's nice and hot and flat. No, Agathe, it's not only the cowboys. You can ride better there and you don't have to duck for the trees."

Maria, who sings second soprano, plays the recorder and viola da gamba, came in to tell us that her parents were waiting for us to join them for lunch downstairs.

In the hotel dining room, The Baroness Maria von Trapp — a tall, strong blue-eyed woman in radiant health — dressed like her daughters and like them, without make-up, firmly pressed our hand then introduced us to the Baron ... a twinkling-eyed man who looked like Santa Claus with a mustache instead of a beard. After ordering lunch (three full courses and double desserts) the Baroness apologized for the somewhat disordered state of the family's belongings, "but we're living on the bus and I'm stumbling over everything," she said.

After lunch, she and her family were going downtown to the headquarters of CARE (Co-operative for American Remittances to Europe) to send more food packages to Austria, the Baroness told us. They had already sent 120 packages, and when the family pig was slaughtered this past fall, "we devoted her fat sides to Austria," quipped the Baroness.

• above left:
The Captain and Johannes: another chess game.

above right:
Visiting New York's CARE headquarters on December 21, 1946. Within a month the von Trapps formed their own Austrian Relief organization.

left:
Backstage rehearsal for the December 22, 1946 concert at Town Hall.

overleaf:
The von Trapps onstage at Town Hall.

119

Page from Route Book tells Story of Conquest of U. S. and Canada by

THE TRAPP FAMILY SINGERS

1945-1946—107 Dates: Tour complete except few dates in Florida.
1946-1947—Now Booking 8th Transcontinental Tour.

Season 1945-46

> New York Times, December 24, 1945:
> "In its à cappella singing the group again inspired admiration by its balanced blending of tone, strict adherence to pitch and careful attention to detail. And us always the work possessed an indescribable charm, with its unpretentious, intimate approach and genuine sincerity."

Exclusive Management: METROPOLITAN MUSICAL BUREAU, INC.
(F. C. Coppicus and F. C. Schang)
Division of COLUMBIA CONCERTS, INC.
113 W. 57th Street, New York 19, N. Y.

ost War
ears
945-1947

*had a seven year hiatus
m medicine. I had been
busy singing to mind,
t something happened:
was as if I was called back
medical life again."*
— *Rupert von Trapp*

*hen one has gifts,
re is also a responsibility
share those gifts."*
— *Werner von Trapp*

*e had to keep up the
ooling of the younger
ldren, so while we traveled
ur bus, schooling went on.
h of us grown-ups taught
nething different in
ry part of the bus.
ne-room schoolhouse!"*
— *Maria von Trapp*

In January 1945, while the *Trapp Family Singers* resumed their tour, Rupert and Werner arrived in Italy with the 10th Mountain Division. The 13,000 men immediately entered combat fighting in the northern Apennine Mountains, surmounting some of the roughest terrain experienced in World War II. The goal was to drive the Germans from Mount Belvedere and nearby peaks where the enemy was entrenched.

Rupert and Werner, like the men of the 10th, were eager to fight the Germans, who considered the Americans inept in dealing with snowy, mountainous conditions. On February 18, a night climb by the Americans took Riva Ridge, surprising the Germans who counterattacked. Werner was in a position to hear the enemy, only yards away, planning an assault. He translated the German commands, allowing his company to shift positions, thus avoiding eight counterattacks.

• **Rupert and Werner gave distinguished service while overseas.**

"Always Forward" was the motto of the 10th Mountain men. They advanced to rid the region of the German stronghold. After six days of fierce fighting the Americans took the last bastion, Mount Belvedere. The way was open to move on to the Alps and further penetrate the heart of the Nazi empire.

Casualties were high. As a medic Rupert evacuated wounded men, using whatever means he could: toboggans, jeeps, or litters. He saved the life of a severely injured comrade.

During the final weeks of the war, the 10th Mountain division fought its way north. By May 5 they reached Nauders, Austria. The German surrender occurred on May 8. The 10th Mountain Division had seen 114 days of combat.

After *Victory in Europe Day*, Rupert and Werner were granted a furlough to investigate the fate of Villa Trapp. They found the family home occupied by American army officers, who were at first reluctant to believe that the von Trapp men had actually once lived there. They wrote to the family in Vermont of the surprising changes they discovered at Villa Trapp. While Heinrich Himmler occupied the house significant renovations were made, with the costs estimated at $150,000.

A bomb shelter was built. A private well and electric plant was installed. A suite was established for Hitler's use. Quarters for guards were constructed. To obscure the house, a forbidding wall enclosed the property. Rupert and Werner learned that the household contents were distributed to Salzburg residents whose homes were destroyed by Allied bombs. The American government rented the property until it reverted to the von Trapps.

In August 1945 Rupert and Werner returned from Europe. The entire *Trapp Family Music Camp* turned out to meet them.

Rupert, using the G.I. Bill of Rights for tuition, resumed medical studies at the University of Vermont. Absent from medicine for so long, he felt the need to repeat course-work he had taken in Austria. His decision to choose medicine over music was permanent. "It was hard for the family to take," he admitted.

• **Homecoming 1945: Werner and Rupert return from military service.**

below right: **Father Wasner tutors Rosmarie in Latin on the bus.**

Werner eventually rejoined the family on tour. Considered one of the most musical siblings, he played cello, viola da gamba, clarinet, and all the recorders. He also composed. Agriculture interested him; between tours he assisted with the family farm. During the war he vowed to build a stone chapel dedicated to Our Lady of Peace if he survived unscathed. He selected a site behind the house, laboring for years to erect the woodland chapel.

In 1946 the *Trapp Family Singers* traveled in a new blue-and-cream-colored General Motors parlor coach bus. The vehicle, which accommodated 37 passengers, was customized as a home on wheels. There was a cot in the rear, and an area for preparing lunches. On the bus, Rosmarie, Lorli, and Johannes were tutored by family members. During the 1946-1947 concert season, the girls finished high school graduation requirements of Mount St. Mary's Academy in Burlington, Vermont.

During their Christmas break from touring the von Trapps were contacted by Major General Harry J. Collins of the 42nd Rainbow Division occupation forces in Salzburg. He described postwar shortages, hunger and desperation of the Austrians, asking the family to aid their homeland through the powerful medium of their concerts. The result was the formation of the *Trapp Family Austrian Relief*, headed by Captain von Trapp.

The winter-spring 1947 tour covered 30,000 miles. "There we discovered that the American heart is unable to see suffering without doing something about it," said Maria von Trapp. At concerts she gave what the family called "Mother's Austrian Relief speech

above: **The 1946-1947 version of the Trapp Family Singers.**

top right: **The Captain and Werner packing shipments to Austria.**

right: **Loading the Jeep for a trip to the Stowe post office.**

below right: **Hedwig and Agathe sort clothing for Austria.**

idiences responded, donating
thing, foodstuffs, and sundry
plies. The bus was sometimes so
immed with contributions that
re was standing room only.
iring long drives between concerts
e von Trapps operated a one-family
ief organization, systematically
paring and shipping supplies to
stria. Over 275,000 pounds of
-saving goods were distributed
U.S. Army chaplains in Salzburg
d Vienna. The family was flooded
th heartfelt letters of thanks. The
ptain was gratified that his old
vy comrades were assisted.
or their charitable work for
stria, the von Trapp family was
arded a Benemerenti medal by

Pius XI in 1949. Since then
Austria has officially recognized
the family's humanitarian efforts.

While the family toured the
West Coast, the weary Captain
often retired to the cot in the rear
of the bus. His persistent cough
was so alarming that he flew from
Seattle to New York where he had
faith in a doctor who had treated
him previously. Maria was so
alarmed by her husband's health
reports that she joined him in
New York. She found the Captain
greatly deteriorated, diagnosed
with lung cancer. Their fervent
desire was to get him home to the
farm on Luce Hill.

The family finished the tour and

• The last family portrait of the von Trapps, at home in Stowe, 1946.
front: **Lorli, Agathe, Johanna, Mother, Johannes, Georg and Rosmarie.**
back: **Werner, Martina, Rupert, Hedwig and Maria.**

• Georg von Trapp.

returned home. The loving father listened to his children's stories of the concerts and collections for Austria. As always he was selfless and quietly heroic. In case he did not recover, he urged: "Please don't bury me with my shoes; send them to the needy in Austria." The Captain wanted no great unhappiness should he die. "Thank God that I have reached my goal," he told his family. The end came for Georg von Trapp during the night of May 30, 1947.

As he wished, he died at home. Family members surrounded him; each received his blessing. In their grief the family honored the father's final wishes. They sang over his body in the flower-filled living room. The Bishop permitted a cemetery consecration just a few hundred feet from the house. On the burial day a procession of family and friends gathered. Frier bore the coffin, wrapped in a flag from the Captain's submarine. Ar Austrian custom was enacted at the grave: mourners sprinkled ho water and soil into the ground.

Agathe, his oldest daughter, summarized her father. "He was hero in warfare and a hero in his everyday living ... a quiet man, bu when he spoke, one listened."

• Art by
Agathe von Trapp.

He lived his life upright, without complaining, always finding things to do which were helpful to his family."

Despite their loss, the family carried on. Summer 1947 was filled with music camp, the farm, Austrian relief work, and a multitude of challenges. There were illnesses, including a near-fatal one for Maria. Of those difficult times Maria observed that "There are times when you don't have to search for the Will of God. You can only bow your head and say, 'Thy Will be done.' While you are sad down to the core of your being, you are also at peace."

• "I *loved* him," said Lorli.
"He was always
self-effacing, putting others
ahead of himself."

• Gravesite of Georg in the family cemetery.

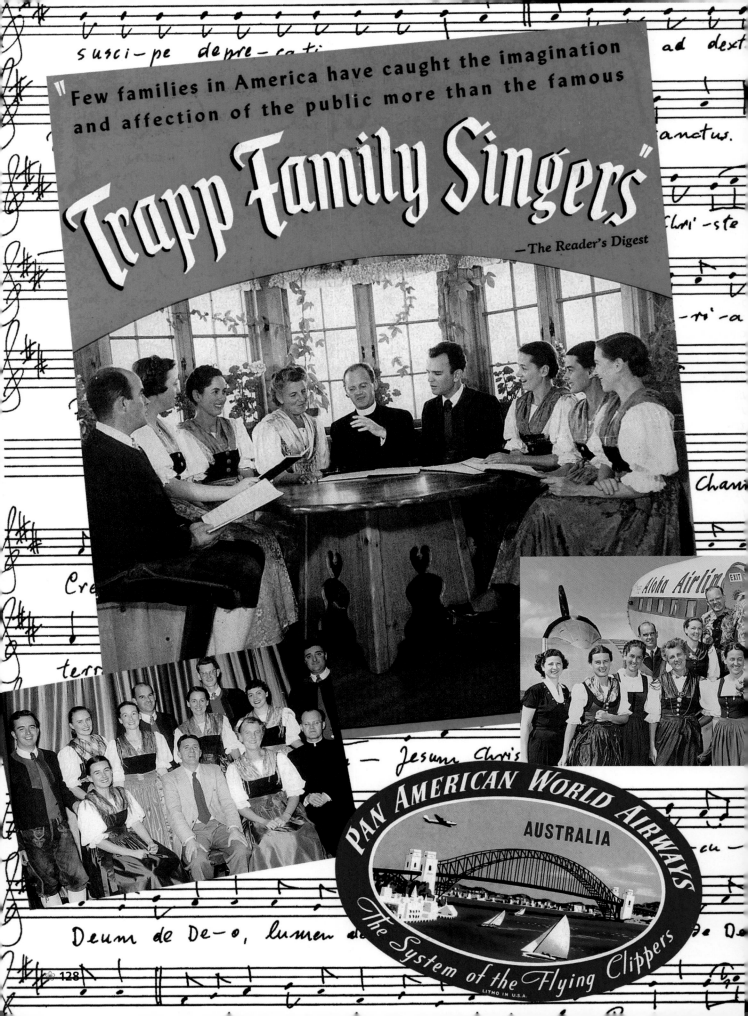

On Wings
and Wheels
1948-1955

*Our music made a great
impression on audiences
around the world, even
in the South Seas.
These native peoples
listened spellbound to
our singing. The value
of the music is in the
music itself; it is immortal.
Music is the language
of the heart."*
— Maria von Trapp

*When the family was
in Italy they sang in Italian;
in France, they sang
in French. They learned to
sing English in America.
Later on in Mexico, they
sang in Spanish.
In Australia, it was
Australian songs.
There were magnificent
landscapes to see;
I really loved that."*
— Rosmarie von Trapp

Following the Captain's death there were significant changes within
the family circle, both personal and professional. Rosmarie no longer
toured. Artistic and musical, she was nevertheless uncomfortable on
stage. "I didn't like singing as much as the others, because I had stage
fright," she recalled. "But Mother loved doing the concerts and
talking to the audiences."

Rupert graduated from medical school just prior to his father's death.
At 34, he was keen to begin his internship and marry his fiancée
Henriette Lajoie. The couple's September 1947 wedding in Fall River,
Massachusetts, was headline news. Since the von Trapp family was
expected to sing, local businesses allowed employee leave time to
witness the nuptials. The church was filled with 3,000 attendees;
the ceremony had the aura of a royal wedding.

• **Rupert and Henriette's wedding in 1947.**

Rupert established his medical practice in the country setting of
Adamsville, Rhode Island, where he spent the bulk of his career.
An early 1800s colonial house became his office and family home.
Rupert's practice thrived, along with his family of six children.
His son George was the first von Trapp grandchild, and the first
von Trapp baby boomer.

• above: **Werner and Erika were married at Cor Unum.**
top left: **Johanna and Ernst's wedding in 1948.**
lower left: **Martina and Jean were wed at Blessed Sacrament Church in Stowe.**

Six months following her brother's wedding, on Easter Monday 1948, Johanna married fellow Austrian Ernst Florian Winter. This concluded her singing career. The Winters and von Trapps shared experiences: Ernst's family also fled Austria post-Anschluss, immigrating to America. After earning a degree at the University of Michigan, Ernst participated in the Normandy invasion. He met Rupert and Werner in the 10th Mountain Division. Among the first American liberators of Austria, Ernst had been asked by Captain von Trapp to check the status of Villa von Trapp.

At Christmas time, 1948, Wern and Erika Klambauer were wed at home in Stowe. Erika, a schoo friend of Martina's in Austria, kn the von Trapps well. She weather the war years with her family nea Salzburg. During a postwar visit Stowe, Erika and Werner became engaged. Following their weddin and a Canadian ski trip, Werner introduced his bride to America when she joined the family on a concert tour.

The Music Camp was the cataly that introduced Martina and a French-Canadian, Jean Dupire. A romance developed and they

re married in 1949 in Stowe.
rtina and her brother Werner
nained in the singing group.
t with four post-World War II
rriages in quick succession,
ria understood "that we knew
s might be the beginning of the
l of our singing together."

illa Trapp, an important family
with Austria, was sold to the
ngregation of the Missionaries
he Precious Blood in 1947.
th the proceeds, debts were
d and two wings were added to
house. Now, when Maria
ited people to "Come see us
towe, Vermont!" there was
ually enough room to entertain
m. When the von Trapps
ght a name for their home,
y settled on "Cor Unum",
aning "one heart." The name
It described the lives of early
ristians who lived cooperatively,
h sharing with the group. Family
among the von Trapps mirrored
t example.

n an auspicious day in May 1948,
mbers of Cor Unum drove to
ntpelier, Vermont to be sworn
as American citizens. Along
h natives of a half-dozen other
untries, the von Trapp family
eated the oath of allegiance.
ey dropped the "von" from their
nes and became simply "Trapps."

AN AUTHOR IS BORN

On a summer evening at the Trapp Family Farm, in a tent lit by a kerosene lamp, Alix Williamson challenged Maria von Trapp to write a book. Alix Williamson was certain that a book about the von Trapps' adventures in Austria and America would successfully promote concerts. Maria shrugged off the suggestion.

Her subsequent introduction to the publishing world occurred at a concert in Philadelphia.

A strategic piece of luggage was accidentally left at the hotel prior to the performance. "To our horror," Maria said, "we'd forgotten the Austrian costumes for the second half. We dragged out the first part of the concert until the audience no longer applauded. Then, in desperation, I went on stage and out of immediate need, I told the audience some amusing stories about our travels." Meanwhile, the Captain hurried to retrieve the needed luggage. "My husband returned; I heard him signal by clearing his throat offstage. I was saved. But not completely. Mr. Bert Lippincott of J.B. Lippincott Publishers came backstage saying he would publish a book of stories like the ones I'd just told. He told me: 'If you can tell stories like that you can write a book.'"

"Later, at home in Vermont, a car arrived. Out came Mr. Lippincott, Mrs. Lippincott, and two little

Lippincotts. He said he had come to stay until I signed a contract. And that is how I came to write The Story of the Trapp Family Singers. *Almost by compulsion."*

Maria dictated the first draft of her book to Hester, her secretary, in six weeks. She wove her family's story into an exciting and romantic tale. In her usual voluble way, she exceeded the suggested length of the manuscript by 50,000 words, which she cheerfully cut and filed away for a possible sequel.

The Story of the Trapp Family Singers, *published in 1949, became the basis for* The Sound of Music.

In coming years Maria continued to write books: Yesterday, Today and Forever *(1952),* Around the Year with the Trapp Family *(1955),* A Family on Wheels: Further Adventures of the Trapp Family Singers *(1959),* Maria: My Own Story *(1972), and* When the King was Carpenter *(1976).*

The newly minted Trapp Family Lodge with three additional wings, circa 1950. Skiers and summer visitors filled the rooms.

The living room and library, a fusion of Austrian and Vermont ambience.

Overleaf:
Summertime at the Trapp Family Farm.

The von Trapps realized that operating the farm with mostly absentee management was not effective. "My mother could see that farming in this climate would not support the family," noted Johannes. So the dairy herd was sold and the barns were razed. A more productive Vermont industry emerged at nearby Mount Mansfield: Alpine skiing. CCC workers had established trails on Mount Mansfield; by 1940 there was a single ski lift. During the post-war era, Stowe established itself as the "Ski Capital of the East." Skiers arrived in droves. They needed beds; when the von Trapps toured, their empty rooms were rented.

"With my nine siblings there were always a lot of people visiting us," said Johannes. "We seldom sat down to dinner with less than eighteen or twenty people. Friends of friends asked to stay with us because they wanted to ski or whatever. We had to start charging. That's how we eased into the hotel business. We formalized it in 1950, becoming the Trapp Family Lodge."

The Lodge was charming and comfortable, and music was everywhere. "I remember times I'd wash pots and pans in the kitchen," Johannes recalled. "Hedwig had been cooking and we'd start singing and harmonizing. Another family member would join us. Soon the guests would leave the tables and come into the kitchen to hear us sing."

The Trapp Family Lodge, as Agathe said, was "Mother's dream come true."

During the 1950s the von Trapps added foreign tours to their travels. From April through June 1950 the family concertized through Central and South America. They sang for audiences in Mexico, Guatemala, and Panama. They continued through the Caribbean Islands and Venezuela. They performed in Brazil and Argentina. They flew across the Andes for concerts in Chile, Ecuador, Peru, and Colombia.

• During a post-World War II growing season on the Trapp Family Farm production included 100 tons of hay, 20 acres of silage corn, 80 bushels of apples, 200 pounds of honey from three hives, 180 bushels of potatoes, 500 pounds of milk per day, enough fresh and processed vegetables to last a year, and 500 pounds of pork. The sugar bush produced from 300-1000 gallons of maple syrup, depending on weather and sap flow. The farm animals included 30 cows, a bull, 12 heifers, 35 sheep, 2 horses and 50 pigs.

"We loved working on the gardens, fields and meadows," said daughter Maria. "During the maple sugaring period, if we were not on concert tour, we helped father collect the sap."

• **A promotional photo used for the South American and European tours in 1950.**
l-r: **Father Wasner, Martina, Agathe, Maria, Mother, Johannes, Hedwig, Werner, Rosmarie and Lorli.**

South American audiences were warmly appreciative. "Rio de Janeiro was great," Werner remembered. "We had eleven curtain calls." One admirer searched for the perfect compliment. "You biggest mother in world!" he told Maria.

Lorli turned nineteen during the tour. She recalled the excitement of frequent flights, exploring jungles, and the thrill of singing in the Teatro Colón in Buenos Aires. "The theater is a duplicate of La Scala in Milan," Lorli recalled. "It was so special to sing there because our voices floated automatically with the perfect acoustics. Backstage, after our second concert, the Austrian conductor of 'The Magic Flute' came up to Father Wasner saying, 'I hope you know what you have in

this choir; it is like one instrument.'"

During the tour Father Wasner filled fifteen pounds of manuscript paper with folk songs from Brazil, Chile, and Argentina. He continually sought indigenous music to include in future concerts.

At eleven, Johannes was already a budding naturalist. He pressed examples of South American flora and fauna in books, and acquired a Peruvian ostrich egg. In Panama City he found an eight inch scorpion, preserving it in a bottle of cologne. He coaxed his reluctant mother to join him in visiting a sanctuary for poisonous snakes. "I found these trips fun," he said. "I was young so I didn't notice what a hard schedule it was for my family."

The *Trapp Family Singers* presented

61 concerts before returning to Stowe to conduct the 1950 Music Camp sessions.

In August the family sailed to Europe for a concert tour. Their first stop was Austria. After twelve years of absence it was an emotional return.

Maria remembered the oppositi_ from friends and relatives when s_ and the Captain led the family ou_ of Austria in 1938. "We knew we had to leave. Now we returned to a bombed-out Austria. People had lost everything, including their sons, for Hitler. Doing the Will of God is like walking in a dark tunnel. Then comes a blinding light and you know you were right_

Because of the impact of the Austrian Relief, the von Trapps

• right: **The return to Salzburg included a concert on the Cathedral Squa_**

• **Martina rehearses** (third from right) **with the family in the bay window at Cor Unum not long before her unexpected death.**

were given heroic welcomes.

In Salzburg they found the old city marked by American influences due to the presence of United States occupation forces. Daughter Maria said, "It was a shock to see the changes. There were even Coca-Cola billboards around. And Salzburg was expanding too."

Patching together the old and the new, the family was invited to reside at Villa Trapp during their stay. There they salvaged their remaining belongings. Important items were shipped to Stowe. The rest was auctioned.

The Trapp Family Singers gave three performances during the Salzburg Festival. The tour then continued through Italy, Germany, Belgium, France, Sweden, Denmark, Norway, Wales, and England. The year concluded with the usual Christmas concerts and a live radio broadcast on Christmas Eve.

When the family departed for a West Coast tour in January 1951, Martina remained at home. She and her husband Jean were expecting their first child. Martina followed the family's daily itinerary and wrote to them regularly. When she learned that Werner's young daughter Barbara was introduced on the stage, she was delighted. She wrote: "That must have been cute! Oh, I can imagine it so well ..." Martina missed the concerts, but anticipated motherhood.

In February, while in California, Maria received shocking news. As she related, "The telephone rang and Jean said 'Mother, Martina is dead.'" She had died in childbirth along with her daughter Notburga. The family sang a requiem for their sister in a California church, unable to return home together. Concerts continued; only Mother could be in

Vermont with Rupert and Rosmar[ie] when Martina and her child were buried close to the Captain.

—

With so many von Trapps missi[ng] from the choir, talented musician[s] were hired. Tenor Donald Meissn[er] sang for two years. Virginia Farri[s] toured for a season. Johannes spe[nt] 1952-1953 in boarding school, on hiatus from singing while his sopra[no] voice morphed into a baritone.

Hal and Charlene Peterson wer[e] recruited from the Music Camp during that period. As Maria explained, "One afternoon Fathe[r] Wasner said, 'wouldn't it be wonderful if we had people like this in our group?' 'Well, why not ask them,' I said. I still remember the place where I stopped Charlene and asked her if they could join t[he] Trapp Family Singers. 'But I don['t] think we are good enough,' she said. The truth is that they are bo[th] very, very good musicians and ha[ve] enhanced our group ever since."

The *Trapp Family Singers* gave concerts in the Hawaiian Islands in 1952 and 1953. Returning to California from the second tour, the group stopped for two days with Bob Hope's family who had previously vacationed at Cor Unu[m.] The von Trapps attended a Hollywood party for the comedi[an's] fiftieth birthday. Hal Peterson wrote his mother: "Char and I ju[st]

ood around and stared, for there
ere radio and movie stars all over
e place. Later in the evening
e sang a few songs, and a little
npromptu show was put on.
Irs. Hope sang. Jerry Colonna
d routines; Bob heckled him
om the sofa. Char sang a duet
th Fred MacMurray. It was
ally a wonderful evening."

• **Lorli wearing a traditional Hawaiian muumuu.**
The Newman Club presented the entire family with native clothing, which they wore during concerts on the Islands.

below:
The family on the famous S.S. Lurline in 1952, en route to Hawaii. far left:
Maria's secretary, Hester; Johannes, Werner, Fathers McDonough and Wasner, Hedwig, Mother.
top: **Rosmarie, Lorli, Agathe, Maria.**

Father McDonough from Blessed Sacrament Church in Stowe traveled with the von Trapps. When they sang at church services, Father McDonough quipped, "We have the best church choir in America!"

HOW I JOINED THE TRAPP FAMILY SINGERS

by Annette Brophy Jacobs

• Annette and Maria in 1994; lifelong friends.

During my second year of study at Juilliard School of Music, my voice teacher, Madame Marion Freschl, asked me to travel to Stowe to audition for the Trapp Family Singers. They were preparing for a tour of New Zealand and Australia, followed by another USA tour. I would replace one of the daughters, Lorli, who had recently married. The choir badly needed a first soprano.

I was torn between two yearnings: to continue studying, or to meet the famous von Trapps. I had already read about them in The Story of the Trapp Family Singers. I decided to go to Stowe.

March 10, 1955: A beautiful black limousine called for me at Madame Freschl's apartment. A lovely, smiling, rosy-cheeked young woman, clad in a dirndl, greeted me. She hugged me and introduced herself: "I am Maria von Trapp, but the family calls me Mitzi, and you may do so, too."

Maria had a lovely, musical laugh and was warm and chatty. I liked her immediately. We collected Werner and his wife Erika at the Wellington Hotel, and started the long drive to Stowe. We got acquainted on the ride, arriving at midnight.

March 11, 1955: I met the rest of the family the next morning. Father Wasner handed me music and sat down at the piano. We all started to sing. I was shaking in my boots, sight-reading the score, alone on my soprano part. I was actually singing with the Trapp Family Singers!

After rehearsal, I sang alone ... selections from Mozart and Schubert. Father Wasner was an amazing pianist. I was singing for someone with profound talent, the kind of musician I never dreamed of meeting.

After rehearsals Maria took me to the sugar house near the Trapp Family Lodge. Sap collected from the maple trees was being boiled. There I met Alvaro Villa, a bass singer who had joined the family choir.

March 12, 1955: Baroness Maria von Trapp appeared. She told me to call her "Mother." She had been in St. Johnsbury, Vermont, working in seclusion on two books. The tall, elegant woman greeted me with a warm smile and a kiss. She immediately wanted to hear me sing. I sang an aria from "The Magic Flute." When I finished, Mother told me: "That isn't the sort of thing I wanted, but I like your voice. I will listen to you tomorrow in rehearsal."

March 13, 1955: Anxiety flooded over me at Sunday mass in the family's chapel. Could I measure up to their expectations? Did I want to go on tour for a full year? Would my scholarship at Juilliard still be there on my return? God helped me; my nerves calmed enough to carry me through the next rehearsal.

When we finished, the family retired to Mother's quarters for a meeting. They left me alone in the rehearsal

room. When they came downstairs, Mother took me aside. She announced that the family voted unanimously that I should join them on tour. They could only pay me a small stipend per week, room and board, plus all expenses. She said they were in debt, but if the tour was successful, I could expect more money later on.

I was thrilled and humbled, and said I would go. Where else could I learn so much, from people I already loved. Right away, Hedwig whisked me off to measure me for the new Austrian wardrobe I would wear onstage, and off. Hedwig was a talented seamstress, and made most of the family's clothing. Skiers, who were staying at the Lodge, offered me a ride back to New York City that evening. I had just a few days to pack, apply for a passport, and say farewell to my friends and teachers. I needed to return quickly, to rehearse for the tour, which started in May.

March 17, 1955: All was white and beautiful and cold when I returned to Vermont. There had been a big blizzard. Alvaro met me at the train station; we had a bumpy, freezing jeep ride over mountains to Trapps. I stepped in the door, and everyone kissed and greeted me warmly. I felt as if I had returned home.

My new bedroom was two doors from the chapel. At bedtime, I stopped by to sit in the darkness. Only a flickering red candle was burning. God had given me this opportunity. I vowed to be the best person and singer I could be.

So began my year with the Trapp Family Singers. I was a non-Trapp heading for a musical adventure with the von Trapps.

LIFE WITH THE VON TRAPPS
by Barbara Stechow Harris

In 1953 my parents allowed me to travel from Oberlin, Ohio to the Trapp Family Music Camp in Vermont. I was fifteen-going-on-sixteen. I received a partial scholarship in exchange for setting tables, clearing them, and changing beds. I worked hard, but joined the singing sessions for five hours daily. The Trapps had developed charming quarters for campers and their families; 110 people could be accommodated at each "Sing Week." The complex had a chapel, a dining hall and updated kitchen.

Oh, the wonderful food from that kitchen! My favorite memory was the camp cook making apple strudel for all. She started with a handful of dough in the middle of a picnic table, stretching it to cover the whole surface. A mixture of apples, raisins, sugar and cinnamon was rolled up meticulously in layers of paper-thin dough. The result was scrumptious. After each ten day "Sing Week" there were a few days for us workers to catch up on sleep, hike, shop in Stowe, and organize for the next session. We also rounded up friends to "jam" on chamber music, sight-read, and sing folk songs and madrigals. This is how the Trapps came to know me. My family's European roots no doubt influenced my love for their music and traditions. I returned for the 1954 camp season, and attended Lorli's wedding. The family needed someone to fill in for her on their next tour. They took a chance on this teenager! From 1954-1956 I traveled on tours across America, and to Australia and New Zealand.

At home at Cor Unum there was another wedding in June 1954, when Lorli and Hugh Campbell were married in the Music Camp chapel. They met in 1947, working together in the camp kitchen. Lorli's commitment to singing was deep, but she likewise felt a calling to be a wife and mother. Her beautiful soprano voice and cheery, uplifting disposition were keenly missed by the family.

Early in 1955 an announcement was mailed out, saying "There will be no *Trapp Family Music Camp* this summer, because we go to Australia and New Zealand! Our home will be open to guests and we are looking forward to a grand reunion at the *Music Camp* in 1956."

Johannes called the New Zealand-Australia tour "our longest and most exciting trip." Six months of performances were booked, often with two concerts each day. In preparation, Father Wasner assembled five separate musical programs to vary the repertoire during extended stays in cities. Rehearsals occupied March and April. Four non-Trapp singers joined the personnel: Barbara Stechow, Annette Brophy, tenor Peter La Manna, and bass Alvaro Villa. When Maria gave her introductions on stage she said, "I made one sweeping gesture and called everyone my family."

• **Lorli and Hugh's wedding at the Music Camp Chapel.**
Photo courtesy of Barbara Harris

Father Wasner felt it wise to bolster the choir with the extra, trained voices. "We were traveling far, and it seemed right," he said. For the non-Trapps, as they were dubbed, singing with the von Trapps was a life-changing experience. Alvaro, immersed in their lives of music, prayer and work for two years, summed it up: "My life was divided in two ... before meeting the Trapps, and after meeting the Trapps."

Prior to the tour departure, Werner struggled with loyalty to the singing family and his duty as a husband and father. "There were certain duties only I could perform during the concerts," he said. A concert reviewer noted his indispensable qualities: "Workhorse of the ensemble appears to be Werner.

He does a variety of chores in an unassuming style. He sings tenor, plays a liquid-voiced viola da gamba, and yodels."

Werner's fifth child was born just hours before the plane left for the South Seas. It was not easy for him to leave Erika and the children behind.

When the von Trapps disembarked from their long flight in Auckland, New Zealand, they were an immediate sensation. Entertainers from abroad were a rarity in 1955. In New Zealand, the media regularly reported on their peripatetic lives, and touted their musical skills. "The Trapps, both genuine and borrowed, are an endearing group," wrote a Christchurch critic. "They were obliged to give seven encores."

Barbara Stechow, who turned eighteen on the tour, wrote her family of the outstanding reception: "The concert-goers have a really wonderful custom ... they wait after a concert outside the theater doors and give a last 'three cheers' for the artists. We always feel really appreciated. Almost every night in Christchurch this custom caused a traffic jam, with people crowding all around our bus to hear our last encore, usually 'Brahms Lullaby'."

New Zealand offered the von Trapp family a chance to explore native culture and folkways when they visited a Maori *pa*. They heard the native chants and songs, and discovered the intricate poi dance.

• **Rehearsing with Father Wasner at Cor Unum for the 1955 Australian-New Zealand tour.**
l-r: **Father Wasner, Peter LaManna, Barbara Stechow, Johannes, Annette Brophy, Hedwig, Mother, Maria, Werner, Agathe, and Alvaro Villa.**

• **En route to New Zealand, the the von Trapps and the non Trapps gave a concert in Honolulu.** Photo courtesy of Annette B. Jacobs

e poi dance found its way into
app Family concerts, as well as
aori melodies with arrangements
Father Wasner. He also created a
rring arrangement of *Waltzing
atilda* in anticipation of the
stralian concerts.

he tour of Australia took the
pp Family Singers to the out-
ck's smaller cities, in addition to
grandest theaters in Melbourne,
isbane, Adelaide, and Sydney.
ey experienced the Aboriginal
lture and saw kangaroo, koala,
d wallaby. They performed for
ousands of schoolchildren, and
n re-created their Christmas
icert in Melbourne's Town Hall.
uring the New Zealand-
stralia concert tour, the family
lized, as Mother Trapp said,
was time to say *auf Wiedersehen*
ur melodies together, but never
the wonder of our memories
l fine music."

• **The final version of the Trapp Family Singers in Australia.**
l-r standing: **Father Wasner, Alvaro Villa, Peter LaManna, Johannes, Hedwig, Werner, Mr. Baldwin (Tour Manager), Barbara Stechow.** front: **Maria, Mother, Annette Brophy, Agathe.**

The von Trapps were entertained by Maori singers and dancers.
Father Wasner incorporated indigenous songs into
the family's concerts. Maria, Barbara, and Annette learned
the native poi dance, demonstrating it on stage.
They promised to introduce the intricate movements
at the Music Camp. "Now is the Hour" (*Po Atarau*),
a farewell song to Maori soldiers during World War I,
became part of the Trapp Family repertoire.

• **Two Marias and Johannes**

chapter 14

New Directions for the von Trapps

"Twenty years is a long time to stand on the stage and sing."
— Werner von Trapp

"Our singing lasted long, and turned out unbelievably well, but it was time to lead quieter lives."
— Dr. Franz Wasner

"My husband had not wanted us to forget: in the adventure of faith there is no such thing as a last encore. 'Whenever God closes a door, He opens a window.'"
— Maria von Trapp

Left:
From 1952-1959, working alone in his spare time, Werner constructed the "Our Lady of Peace" stone chapel near the Trapp Family Lodge. The chapel is a hiking destination and woodland sanctuary for Lodge visitors.

Disbanding the *Trapp Family Singers* was a difficult decision. For twenty years the group sang for millions in over 2,000 concerts through thirty countries. The finale came in December 1955 and January 1956: the Farewell Tour. The last New York City appearances were three pre-Christmas concerts at Town Hall, where the von Trapps were perennial favorites, appearing there more than forty times through the years.

The final concert of the *Trapp Family Singers* was in January 1956, before an overflow audience in Concord, New Hampshire. As the family took their final bows, Father Wasner expressed a collective wish: "We hope that what we have done will carry on, out into the world."

The *Trapp Family Music Camp* was discontinued after the 1956 summer sessions. "It was time to step out on our own," Agathe said.

By year's end, Maria, Rosmarie, and Johannes accepted an invitation to serve as lay missionaries in Papua New Guinea. Their mother and Father Wasner left Vermont with them to join a fact-finding group who was gathering data on the status of missions in the South Pacific. The three children were stationed on Fergusson Island, working with two priests, three nuns, and an island teacher.

The three siblings lived as the islanders did, in huts made with bush materials, without running water, power, or ready communication with the outside world. Their first link with the native people was through music. "We sang and folk danced," recalled Maria. "Language was no barrier. We formed two choirs, and sang songs we had used in our concerts!" Maria said. She adapted Palestrina motets, Bach chorales, and Gregorian chant to native melodies and discovered that the villagers were very musical. As Rosmarie observed: "Music is always a wonderful way to be friendly and create peace."

While Maria and Rosmarie taught English to 72 elementary students, seventeen-year-old Johannes learned the Dobu language quickly. He became "village brother" to residents. He worked with area men to build a house for his sisters, a chapel, and a school from timber dragged through the water from nearby islands. He swam, fished, and hunted wild pigs with the locals. "When Johannes came, he was a boy to the natives," said Maria.

• Leaving for New Guinea for the first time, 1956. l-r: **Rosmarie, Mother, Johannes, Maria, and Father Wasner.**

"When he left he was a man to them."

On the first island Christmas Eve, the von Trapps and the congregation gathered on the grass outside the little church. "*Silent Night* and the other old favorites sounded strangely exotic in Dobu," Maria recalled, "but never more joyful. I knew on that night I had never experienced a more festive Christmas." Linking past and present, Johannes tuned his radio to the BBC — and out came Christmas carols — by the *Trapp Family Singers.*

Mother Trapp visited her children with stories of her own to tell. With the "Flying Bishop" (Reverend Arckfeld), she and Father Wasner saw incredible sights as they journeyed by plane and boat. "In one village I was the first white woman the tribal headhunters ever saw. They were the first headhunters I ever saw! So we were mutually astonished. One village had just eaten the other. A ring of these natives confronted

me just as I realized my nylons were twisted around my legs. I stooped over to straighten them, when with one voice the natives uttered a frightening grunt. Headhunters, I thought. This is it! But the chief politely asked me to do it again. I thought: Do what again? 'Please white queen,' the interpreter said, 'wiggle your skin again.'"

After a year in the tropics, and a bout with malaria, Maria von Trapp came home. She managed the Trapp Family Lodge and started a new career as a lecturer.

After twenty-four years with the von Trapps, Father Wasner volunteered for missionary work in the Fiji Islands. His assignment was the mission station at Naiserelangi. Father Wasner did outstanding work, building up a rundown mission which overlooked Viti Levu Bay and several picturesque villages. While there he developed a strong interest in recording and preserving Fijian art, music, and culture.

In 1959 Johannes returned to Vermont to enter college. Rosma also came home, stopping in Australia en route to study art.

Maria made mission work her lifetime vocation. In 1961 she too home leave at the Lodge. Mother described Maria's passion: "She eats, drinks, and breathes mission She hasn't changed a bit — the same twinkle in her eyes and the same infectious 'Mitzi-laugh', those ringing scales of laughter, s irresistible that you have to join i

• **Daughter Maria in New Guine with a small Papuan friend.**

When singing ended, the rest o the family scattered, though not far as the mission fields:

Rupert was a beloved Rhode Isla country doctor, active in commun and church. He and his wife Henriette raised six children. She contracted polio early in their married life. With an elevator and customized household, she exper managed child-rearing and book keeping for Rupert's medical pract

• **Hedwig and Maria on the Lodge porch.**

gathe and Mary Lou Kane started we's first kindergarten. Later, y established Sacred Heart dergarten in suburban Baltimore, ryland. Agathe's duties included cting a boy's choir which sang iems and masses in Gregorian nt. Art and music were continuing ences in her life.

erner taught at the Community sic and Arts School in Reading, nsylvania until he bought a y farm near the Vermont village aitsfield in 1959. There he Erika raised their six children. tunately it is only forty minutes from Stowe," said Mother Trapp, "so I rush over every so often. Erika always keeps fresh buttermilk for me and there is no better rye bread than hers."

Hedwig was often in residence at the Trapp Family Lodge, assisting in its operation. "Her joy and energy were contagious," niece Barbara remarked. Hedwig's passion for arts, crafts, and music were perfect credentials for a Catholic Youth Organization job in Honolulu, which she accepted in 1960. She later taught music at St. Anthony's School.

Johanna and husband Ernst Winter raised seven children in America and Austria. In 1960 the family moved to Austria, where Ernst became foundation director and professor at the Diplomatic University of Vienna. The Winter family lived in the castle Eichbüchel, where educational seminars were held, and visiting professors taught. John Irving wrote his first novel at the castle while the Winters managed it.

Rosmarie studied occupational therapy, assisted at Sacred Heart kindergarten, lived and worked at the Trapp Family Lodge, and belonged to a religious community

• **The Lodge in its summer splendor.**

in Pittsburgh. She mastered numerous arts and crafts, and remained an enthusiastic musician.

Lorli and Hugh Campbell raised seven daughters. They remained in New England, living in several locations where Hugh served as teacher, coach, and headmaster. Lorli and Hugh purchased a parcel of Werner's farmland and built a home there. This enabled the two sets of cousins to grow up in close proximity.

Johannes, after his Papua New Guinea experience, graduated from Dartmouth College, concentrating in history and biology. He continued his education at Yale, graduating

with a Master of Forest Science degree. Johannes also served with the National Guard as a medic.

~

Except for holidays, and special events, the only von Trapp in permanent residence at the Lodge was Maria. She fostered a familial feeling among the staff and guests, and created lasting traditions.

During his college vacation in 1962 Johannes was the Lodge's assistant manager. He started a wine cellar and a cozy Tyrolean-style bar. A second dining area, called the South Pacific Room, was opened, decorated with carvings, shells, bows, arrows, masks and

shields from New Guinea.

A swimming pool in a meadow behind the Lodge was added. When Johannes introduced horse back riding for guests, his mother was a regular participant.

Down the road from the Lodge in a farmhouse where Werner and his family once lived, Maria found Vermont's first Viennese-style coffee house. Its large deck looked over panoramic mountain views. The coffee house became a great success with tasty lunches and rich desserts . . . gugelhupf, Black Forest cake, Victoria cake, Linzertorte, and what Maria called "the crown and glory": apfelstrudel.

MY YEARS AT THE TRAPP FAMILY LODGE

Sid Lawson

My brother, Ronald Lawson, worked the front desk at the Trapp Family Lodge during vacations from seminarian studies. When he suggested that I too work there, I applied and was accepted to their team. This was during the early '60s, and the Lodge was open winter, summer and fall. I lived at the Lodge in its beautiful setting. Some of us worked in Reservations; others were waiters, bartenders, busboys or dishwashers. On breaks we would run outside to enjoy the wonderful mountain air. But we were always expected to act with decorum while on duty.

After I was hired, I was asked to refer to Maria as "Mother Trapp," as all Lodge employees were asked to. Mother would walk through the dining room to greet guests, as classical music played. Dinner was served on Blue Danube china dishes. Mother wanted the Lodge dining room to be self-sufficient with home-grown healthy foods, so she invited organic gardening pioneers Scott and Helen Nearing to the Lodge,

seeking their advice. I was their driver. Mother then hired an organic gardener to work directly for the Lodge.

Mother was not known in Stowe as a good driver. She was often seen in her convertible speeding along curvy Vermont roads. I sometimes drove her to events; she said I used the brakes too often! She was charismatic and could be quite dramatic.

Often on Saturday nights, we rolled up the rugs for a dance in St. George's Hall, the big recreation room in the Lodge. Mother loved to dance and everyone was invited, both families and Lodge guests. Musicians and a square dance caller, familiar with international dances, were hired. We danced the Austrian "Laendler", with Mother Trapp showing us the steps. She was a very strong woman, and I think she enjoyed challenging her dance partners as to who was leading. It was all marvelous fun!

I got to know many of the von Trapp family members. Rupert visited us; I remember he had a wonderful outgoing personality. Maria came home, on leave from her mission in

New Guinea; she was so pleasant. Werner and Erika were busy farming but occasionally came to the Lodge. They were a stunning couple; we were in awe of them. Rosmarie was sometimes home, and made incredible apfelstrudel. Hedwig periodically helped run the kitchen ... she was a total delight; I adored her. Johannes and I often worked together when he was home from Dartmouth. We enjoyed each other's company.

In November 1963, during the Vietnam war, I received my draft notification. During basic training at Fort Dix, New Jersey, I mentioned I had just left Vermont, where I had worked for Maria von Trapp. That's all it took; I was directed to Chaplain's Assistant School, and eventually worked for a Post Chaplain. I think Mother guided my time, even in the U.S. Army.

While on leave from active duty one Christmas, I returned to work at the Lodge. Johannes surprised me with a gift of a scarf that had belonged to his father. I still wear it, many decades later.

• "The perfect ending of a family choir is when grandchildren start arriving," said Maria von Trapp. Eventually she was grandmother to twenty-seven. In June she hosted "Family Week" at the Lodge for the far-flung von Trapps. Elizabeth Campbell Peters, Lorli's daughter, recalls: "We swam in the Lodge's pool, lunched in the dining room, and selected a present from the gift shop as our birthday gift. We looked forward to this visit." The 1965 gathering (above) included Hedwig, Johannes, Werner, Mother, Lorli, Rosmarie, Agathe, Maria, and a dozen grandchildren. Rupert's family were also regular guests.

A section of the coffee house included Maria's pet project, the Trapp Family Gift Shop. Along with von Trapp books and recordings, the shop featured unique European art, gifts and handicrafts. Yearly buying trips took Maria to international gift shows in Europe, including sojourns in Austria.

During a 1968 lecture at St. Olaf College in Minnesota, Maria had a brainstorm. Why not hire musical students as singing wait staff during the Lodge's summer season? Lynne Peterson, a St. Olaf junior, assembled a group to present after-dinner concerts. A year later Johannes and Lynne were married at the stone chapel built by Werner. By this time, Johannes was general manager of the Lodge.

"For too many years, I ran the Lodge with my left hand: an emotional mother with no business sense," admitted Maria. Nevertheless, she found relinquishment of her role a challenge. "You're always talking about money," she told Johannes. "We are here to make people happy." Johannes countere "As long as we are not making money we could lose this place and not make anyone happy." Although Johannes anticipated a career in natural resources, he "just couldn't bear to see us lose the Trapp Family Lodge." With creativity and determination, he launched plans to make the family business sustainable.

I am the only completely American member of my family, born and educated here. My family is half Austrian, half American, in varying degrees. I am the youngest, but never really had a childhood; I grew up as a little adult. I was once asked how many children were in our family. My response was: "Only me; the rest are all grown-ups."

I was three when we moved to the farm in Stowe. We had a horse barn and a cow barn. I remember walking behind the cows, afraid of being kicked. My earliest memories are of farming. We had a quiet, strict, disciplined life. Because of that, the old Vermonters in Stowe accepted us.

I started singing when I was four. I made a surprise debut in Boston. I stepped forward on the stage and announced that I would sing "Old Mac Donald Had A Farm," which I'd learned the summer before. I sang. The audience applause was so loud that it scared me. My mother was determined I would sing again the next week in New York. I was thinking I wouldn't. Again the audience roared with approval, because I won the battle with my mother. She had enormous charm, but she was tough.

At seven I was singing soprano in the family concerts. Touring was exciting, some places more so than

• During a vacation from Dartmouth, Johannes and Maria discuss Lodge business.

others. I played recorder solos but never had stage fright; the footlights insulated me. My brothers and sisters had been performing much longer; they were sometimes played out. One year we gave nearly 200 concerts. We wore Austrian clothing, just what the family would wear at home in Austria. I hated it! The only time I felt normal was at the farm, running around in blue jeans.

In smoky, dirty cities, I thought of Stowe and my favorite rocks and places to sit. Those spots were a refuge. I spent all the time that I could in our woods. I was the one who cut down our Christmas trees. I knew where the good ones were, because I was always hunting rabbits and deer.

One winter I went to the one-room school house at the bottom of Luce Hill, a three mile walk from home. That was in third grade. I must have stayed home during a concert tour. I'd sometimes ski down and leave my skis at the bottom of the hill. Next day I'd take a sled and tow the skis back home. I didn't fit in at school. My accent was different; we spoke German at home. There were twelve kids in six grades, but I didn't know what to say to them.

I was mostly home-schooled when we were on tour. During the long hours on the bus I read anything I could find, and tried to get out of my lessons. Maria taught me math. My mother taught me French. Father Wasner was my Latin teacher. He had a brilliant mind. More than teaching me the facts, he taught me how to think. I'm sure that was a challenge to him because I was not a great student.

From my mother I inherited my wanderlust and aptitude for languages. She did a fabulous job developing the Trapp Family Lodge and promoting it. She taught me that if you have a good idea and it is good for guests, you can find a way to create and develop it. This was drilled into me from early on. It is part of my paradigm of life.

chapter 15

New Songs to Sing: The Sound of Music

The Story of the Trapp Family Singers has been translated into *The Sound of Music* so [its] message can reach those [wh]o go to the theater."
— Dr. Franz Wasner

"[Th]e *Sound of Music* is a [ma]sterpiece of movie making. [It d]eals with so many themes [tha]t are fundamental to the [hu]man condition: love of [fami]ly, love of a man and a [wo]man, love of country, [lov]e of home, and [ove]rcoming obstacles."
— Johannes von Trapp

[Juli]e Andrews as Maria in [The] *Sound of Music*.
[Pho]to © Photo Fest

The German film company, Gloria, produced two movies based on *The Story of the Trapp Family Singers* in the late 1950s. The films, *The Trapp Family* and *The Trapp Family in America* were well received throughout the world; in Munich the first movie ran for 24 weeks and in Tokyo for 34 weeks. When Broadway actress Mary Martin saw the film she said, "I knew it was for me." An adaptation of the story was envisioned as a Rodgers and Hammerstein musical play with Mary Martin as Maria.

The real Maria was deep in the tropics on her tour of mission stations when the first flickers of interest were shown in adapting her book for the stage. Since the musical version was intended as a vehicle for Mary Martin, Maria was invited to see the actress perform in *Annie Get Your Gun* in San Francisco. The two developed an excellent rapport, but Maria still shied away from an adaptation.

Finally, producer Leland Hayward followed Maria to Europe, where

• **Mary Martin cavorts with Werner and Erika's children at the Lodge.** Photo © Photo Fest

she was recovering from the malaria she acquired while in the South Seas. He pointed out that royalties would aid the mission work she supported, and Maria agreed. The musical became *The Sound of Music*.

Before rehearsals started in 1959, Mary Martin arrived at the Trapp Family Lodge to prepare for her role. "For two blessed weeks, she studied me!" Maria said. "I'm famous for taking very unladylike long steps and talking with my hands. In walking around the house, I always saw Mary out of the corner of my eye, imitating me." Maria also taught Mary how to folk dance, how to kneel, to cross herself, and play the guitar.

"And I taught her a Texas yodel," Mary Martin recalled. "We decided that I was born in Texas, and she was born in Austria, but underneath we were the same Maria."

• above: **Maria and Mary Martin in 1959. "One of the joys of my life was portraying Maria," said Mary.** Photo © Photo Fest

below: **Mary Martin onstage with the Broadway cast of the von Trapp children.**

Photo © Billy Rose Collection, New York Public Library for the Performing Arts

The Sound of Music opened in New York on November 16, 1959, and depicted Maria's arrival in the von Trapp home, her marriage to the Captain, and the family's escape from Austria. Theodore Bikel portrayed the Captain. "I had not been warned that he would make his entrance in his Captain's uniform," Maria noted. "When he came on, it took my breath away. Seeing Mary Martin as me made me feel funny — sort of awkward."

"All of the important things were true," Maria said of the compacted

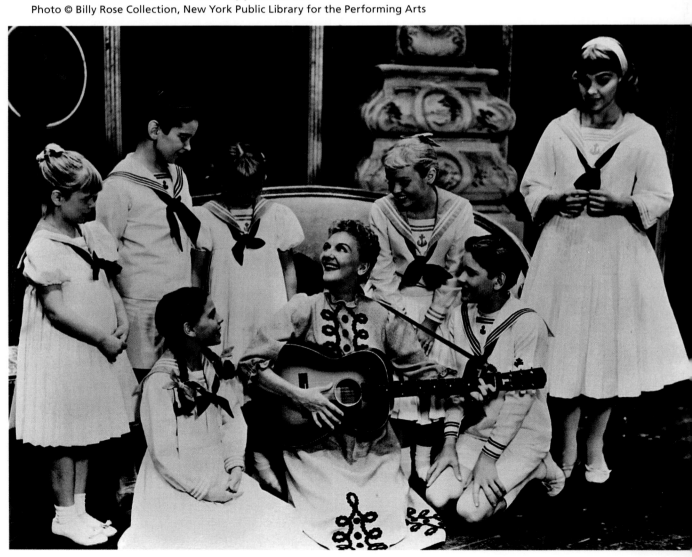

rsion of the von Trapp history. mong the minor changes was the naming of the seven children. odgers and Hammerstein's music the play achieved classic status th such songs as "Climb Ev'ry ountain," "Do-Re-Mi," "My vorite Things," and "The Sound Music."

he musical ran for three years Broadway. Its message of hope, triotism, and family strength had iversal appeal for audiences of all es. "What a role, what a show, at a joy to millions and millions people all over the world!" Mary artin exclaimed.

oon after *The Sound of Music* emiered came a surprise. Maria d, "Like a thunderbolt one day me the invitation that the *Trapp mily Singers* should bring out a ord of *The Sound of Music*. After ch hesitation we finally got seven mbers of the old group together, ed the Juilliard String Quartet d a few additional voices, and de the Warner Brothers record. *Fi Magazine* mentions 'the cellent arrangements and the llful direction of Franz Wasner', d finally calls it 'the finest and st artistic presentation of the re now to be found on records.'" he *Sound of Music* was scheduled become a Twentieth Century Fox ovie, a fact that caused some ncern for Maria. "For heaven's e, what am I going to do if they

have me twice divorced in this film?" she worried. Lorli sympathized with her mother. "We were leery of this news," she said. "We wondered what Hollywood would do with our family of seven daughters!"

Maria had a chance to see the filming of *The Sound of Music* first-hand when she happened to visit Salzburg with family members in

1964. She shook hands with Julie Andrews, who portrayed her, and met Christopher Plummer, who played the Captain. And Maria fulfilled a lifelong wish: she appeared in a movie. During the filming of Julie Andrews' song "I Have Confidence," Maria, Rosmarie, and granddaughter Barbara were instructed to amble across the back-

• **On a visit to Salzburg in 1964, Maria discovered that** ***The Sound of Music*** **was being filmed. Here, she shakes hands with Christopher Plummer (the Captain in the movie version). Also seen is Robert Wise, producer.** Photo © Photo Fest.

How We Appeared in *The Sound of Music* and Other Stories

by Barbara von Trapp Crandall

In 1964, after three years with my maternal grandmother in Salzburg, my family arranged for me to travel back to Vermont. I was fourteen and would be accompanied by my other grandmother, Maria von Trapp, and Aunt Rosmarie. "Mutter", as Maria was known by in our family, was the second mother of my father, Werner von Trapp. The plan was for us to tour Italy and travel by ship from Naples to New York.

Mutter rented a small convertible. We drove into the center of Salzburg where we met the cast and crew filming The Sound of Music. *Director Robert Wise and his staff were nervous about meeting "the real Maria." We all shook hands. Mutter chatted with Julie Andrews and Christopher Plummer and other actors. She also made it known that she had always dreamed of being in movies. As a courtesy, Robert Wise said we could be extras in the scene being filmed. We three were instructed to walk behind the arches on the Domplatz. Julie Andrews ambled through the arches, swinging her guitar, and singing "I Have Confidence."*

Each time we walked behind her, something went awry. We repeated the scene at least sixteen times. Rosmarie and I agreed filmmaking was not an aspiration of ours. But we can be seen for a few seconds during this segment of the movie.

Our trip continued through southern Austria and northern Italy. We spent a few days on the mountain slopes with farmers who were friends from Mutter's youth. This is where Mutter broke her ankle. With her vacation hampered, Rosmarie and I were sent into cathedrals and chapels to pray while Mutter waited in the car. We visited Florence, Sienna, and Assisi, where I fell in love with St. Francis and his way of life. In Rome we stayed at a convent where all the nuns seemed like Mutter's friends.

Somehow, Mutter managed to show us highlights of Rome. Then our trip continued to Naples, with stops at Pompeii and the Isle of Capri.

On our voyage across the Atlantic, Mutter was constantly surrounded by people wanting her advice or attention. One day it was announced that Austrian "knoedl" was on the menu, made by Maria von Trapp! I was unaware that she could cook. I felt nervous for her as we were ushered into the kitchen to help make these dumplings. With some explanation from Mutter, the cooks actually produced them.

What was Mutter like as a grandmother? Certainly not the cuddling kind who knitted sweaters or baked cookies. Instead, she had convictions of faith and strength. She was a great part of the puzzle that made her family's life work. I see her as the engine that pulled the family forward. She brought concert audiences messages of hope — despite her own hardships and illnesses during the touring years. She would not give up. I think her love of God was the legacy she left us.

ground. The short scene was repeate many times, so Maria decided, "Right then and there I knew I ha no talent to be a film actress!"

The Sound of Music was an incredible success when it was released in 1965, and it catapulted the von Trapp family into a renown they had never sought nor expected. But family members were little affected by the movie. When Rupert attended the opening he paid for his own tickets. He thought the movie was "all wet," since he was portrayed as the eldes daughter. When asked who he wa in the film, he affected a mock curtsy and answered, "Liesl."

Agathe preferred to retain her own memories rather than see the movie but finally viewed it twice. It took her sister Maria four years and a ten-hour boat ride to see *The Sound of Music* in New Guine Rosmarie's reaction was, "Wow! Is this my life? It was much different from what I remember living."

The entire family agreed that sta; and screen characterizations of their father were inaccurate, showir him as stern and autocratic. His kind and loving nature was not emphasized. The Captain's daught Maria said she eventually became reconciled to the film version because, "It did show that my fath had great principles."

The Sound of Music became one of the most popular movies ever mad

Die Trapp-Familie *in Amerika*
Ein Divina-Farbfilm der Gloria

- above: *The Sound of Music* von Trapp cast was: Nicholas Hammond (Friedrich), Kym Karath (Gretl), Angela Cartwright (Brigitta), Julie Andrews, Christopher Plummer, Charmian Carr (Liesl), Heather Menzies (Louisa), Duane Chase (Kurt), Debbie Turner (Marta).

Photo © Alamy

The Sound of Music is the most successful movie musical of all time. Domestic box office gross exceeds one billion dollars, adjusted for inflation. It is seen in dozens of languages. The film was shown in Communist China, one of five foreign movies permitted there.

- left: **Two German films preceded *The Sound of Music*.**

It won five Oscars: Best Picture, Editing, Sound, Director, and Score.

Because of its financial success the movie was sometimes dubbed "The Sound of Money." "But not for us," Maria claimed. Due to an early sale of the rights to her book, only a tiny fraction of the profits ever reached the family.

In the summer of 1965, the community of Stowe paid tribute to the von Trapp Family. During the Stowe Festival of Music, the *Trapp Family Singers* performed a rare reunion concert on the meadow near the Lodge. Before a large audience they sang under Father Wasner's direction for the first time in nearly a decade. A White House citation from then President Lyndon B. Johnson recognized the event:

"It is a pleasure for me to join music lovers everywhere in this richly deserved salute to the von Trapp Family. May the music of this Festival echo Vermont's pride in the countless selfless and rewarding accomplishments of the von Trapp Family, and may the praise and gratitude which they have so rightly earned resound throughout our land. Their characteristic devotion to justice and individual dignity, their compassion and dedication to humanity will live forever in the cherished musical legacy which they brought to our shores."

The Sound of Music propelled Maria von Trapp into the life of a

• right:
Maria was a popular and inspiring lecturer.

below:
Reunion Concert: Lorli, Agathe, Maria, Rosmarie, Hedwig, Mother, Johannes, Werner, and Father Wasner.

famous celebrity. "I had expected to lead a quiet life on a Vermont hill, just dealing with our guests," she observed. Instead, she was recognized wherever she went and was heavily booked as a speaker. She was interviewed on numerous television shows, including those of Dinah Shore and Mike Douglas. She became one of Phil Donahue's favorite guests, and made repeated visits to his talk show.

During the summers in Stowe, thousands of tourists arrived at the Trapp Family Lodge hoping to meet "The real Maria from *The Sound of Music*." Maria made

regular appearances in the Gift Shop, patiently signing autographs and posing for photographs. "In times like ours," Maria said, "so filled with 'un-love,' if I can be instrumental in making people happy, this is a great privilege. If *The Sound of Music* or a book of mine has helped them and change their lives, then I feel I wouldn't want it any other way. The million and millions of people who have seen *The Sound of Music* are gettin this message: 'The most precious thing in life is to find out what is the Will of God, and then go do it

How Do I Like *The Sound of Music*?

by Maria von Trapp

After The Story of the Trapp Family Singers was published, Hollywood wanted to buy the movie rights. They were not interested in the real story; they wanted to buy the title and make their own story. This we could not do, and that seemed to close the issue. Years passed; Broadway became interested, and in the late 1950s the stage rights were sold. The Sound of Music became a great success on the stage.

Then I learned from a newspaper that Hollywood was working on a movie version. I was never consulted about this. I had only one wish as far as the movie went. That was to have my husband better represented than he had been in the play. There, he was almost a Prussian general, whistling and shouting commands to his children. I called the producer in Hollywood. When I started to explain that my husband had really been a very kind person, he interrupted me with "Oh, we are not interested. We want to make our own story." Bang! He hung up.

When the movie version of The Sound of Music was finished, I asked for a private showing. My son Johannes and a few friends accompanied me to a private theater in New York. When the lights went out, my heart started beating fast. I found myself suddenly in the mountains around Salzburg. There were those emerald-green meadows I knew so well.

Then I saw myself, played by Julie Andrews, singing "The hills are alive with the sound of music" ... What a strange sensation, to relive my own life on the screen.

I really relived it! ... the time in the convent when I really tried to be a good nun, until the Reverend Mother asked me a momentous question: "Maria, what is the most important thing in life?" I answered: "The most important thing is to find out the Will of God and go and do it." Then I found out that Captain von Trapp was looking for a teacher for one of his children. The nuns decided to send me. This made it appear to me to be the Will of God.

When the Nazis came into Austria, all was changed. We again had to find out what was the Will of God. Should we keep our material goods, or our spiritual goods: our faith and honor? As I sat there watching the film I didn't even notice how odd it was that Hollywood had placed a high mountain in the middle of Salzburg. As we went up one side during our flight from the Nazis, we were in Austria; on the other side we descended into Switzerland, singing "Climb Every Mountain" at the top of our lungs. When you flee, you must do it quietly, I thought. But we must allow Hollywood to do a little Hollywooding. Slowly I came out of the movie and back to the theatre. My face was wet with tears. My anxieties were over. Did I like the film, I was asked. I answered: "Yes, very much indeed."

"The Sound of Music made my grandmother keenly aware that she was a celebrity. She always dressed in her signature Austrian dirndl, which made her easily recognizable to Lodge guests who wanted to meet and talk with her."
— Elizabeth Campbell Peters

Come and join me as I tell you the beginnings of the **Original Sound of Music Tour** in Salzburg, Austria! Salzburg Panorama Tours® is the name of the company which offers this extraordinary tour. When it was founded in 1954 it was called "Kleinbusse Mirabell." In 1964 20th Century Fox was in Salzburg to film The Sound of Music. At that time the film company rented four mini-busses from Salzburg Panorama Tours® to use during filming of the movie. During this time nobody dreamed that this movie would become one of the most famous and successful films ever.

After The Sound of Music's premiere in 1965, the first film fans arrived in Salzburg seeking locations where the story had been filmed. Drivers of the Panorama Tours® had escorted the actors and the film staff to the movie sites during production. They knew the exact locations and shared anecdotes of the actual making of the movie. At that time the Original Sound of Music Tour® was born. I, Stefan Herzl, the Salzburg Panorama Tours® CEO, cherish my personal friendship with the von Trapp Family. During a 1985 visit to the Trapp Family Lodge in Stowe, Vermont, I met many members of the family. In 1998 Maria von Trapp, the Captain's daughter, was in Salzburg and joined our Original Sound of Music Tour® for the first time. She returned numerous times, enjoying the tour on each and every visit. Her siblings, and the movie von Trapps also visited Salzburg periodically.

In 1987 movie director Robert Wise and Julie Andrews were in Salzburg filming a show called "The Sound of Christmas." The mini-busses were involved again. Julie Andrews joined one of our tours, which showed her the filming locations once again. Christopher Plummer followed her in 1998, taking a private tour of Salzburg and the vicinity. In 2000 all seven actors who portrayed the von Trapp children met in Salzburg to film a documentary.

The fiftieth anniversary of The Sound of Music in 2015 brought Julie Andrews again to Salzburg. She filmed an ABC television

• **Stefan Herzl presents Maria w** a long-lost copy of her father' book, inscribed to Hans Schwei the family's butler at Villa Trap He died in Russia during the Battle of Stalingrad. Photo © Stefan Herzl

documentary to commemorate the occasion. A gala anniversary even was held at the Summer Riding School in Salzburg, attended by Johannes and Lynne von Trapp, five of the children from the film, and other dignitaries.

To this day, the fascination for Th Sound of Music remains unbroker Every year, thousands of guests fro all over the globe follow the footste of the actual von Trapp family, an the beloved film actors who portray them...The Original Sound of Mus Tour® is proud to enable visitors as they discover the beauties of the Salzburg region.

• **The Original Sound of Music®** **tour bus.** Photo © Stefan Herzl

• top: **The Castle Leopoldskron in Salzburg is a rococo palace landmark dating to the 1700s. Ten outdoor scenes of** *The Sound of Music* **were filmed there. The historic structure now serves as a hotel.**
Photo ©Tourismus Salzburg

center: **The Pferdeschwemme — The Horse Pond of Salzburg.**
Photo ©Tourismus Salzburg

right: **A famous Austrian gastronomical delight, Salzburger Nockerl.**
Photo ©Tourismus Salzburg

• left:
Because of the unsuitability of the actual Villa Trapp as a filming site, Frohnburg Castle was used to represent the von Trapp family home in movie scenes.
Photo ©Tourismus Salzburg

below: **St. Peter's Cemetery is the oldest cemetery in Austria still in use, and the burial site of Father Wasner**
Photo ©Tourismus Salzburg

right: **The gazebo scene where the movie version's eldest daughter Liesl dances with Rolf, the telegram delivery became a cult classic with filmgoers. A gazebo replica now stands at Hellbrunn Park, reminiscent of the song "Sixteen Going on Seventeen"**
Photo ©Tourismus Salzburg

bove: **The Residenzplatz is a square in the old section of Salzburg. In The** *Sound of Music* **Maria sang** *Have Confidence* **here as she made her way to the Villa Trapp from Nonnberg Abbey.** Photo ©Tourismus Salzburg

bove-below right: **The exterior of the Collegiate Church of St. Michael at Mondsee, near Salzburg, was the site f the movie version of the wedding of Captain Von Trapp and Maria. The majestic baroque interior of the hurch's altars, its sculptures and art works are regional treasures.** Images used under license from Shutterstock.com

Chapter 16

Loss and Triumph: A New Lodge

"The Trapp name is almost a trademark. Stowe is not just another ski area or summer resort, but home of the von Trapps. This has been wonderful for Stowe."
— Herb Hillman,
Stowe hotelier

"The Trapp Family Lodge is meant to be a reflection of my family, not of 'The Sound of Music'. I love the reality of my family's story. The Lodge is us; the movie is the movie."
— Johannes von Trapp

Right:
"On a bitterly cold Sunday winter day, with Christmas 1976 on our doorstep, Johannes is driving the sleigh, his children behind him, with Lynne and myself on the back seat, and behind us, you see the Trapp Family Lodge."
— Maria von Trapp

During winter breaks from concerts, the Captain, Maria, and the children skied on their mountain property. At age four, Johannes joined them. "My favorite way to ski was to loosen the heels on my alpine bindings while on the old roads and trails surrounding our home. It was more like snowshoeing than cross-country skiing, and great exercise. I enjoyed cross-country skiing and would come home from Dartmouth with friends to ski."

Eager to attract more winter guests to the Lodge, Johannes thought of introducing people to Nordic skiing. Starting small, with Norway's Per Sørli to supervise the cross-country ski operation, the enterprise thrived. The Trapp Family Cross-Country Ski Center opened, the first of its kind in America. Old logging roads, trails, and bridle paths on the Lodge land were developed for back-to-nature skiers seeking an alternative to downhill. The von Trapps' 2600 acres of forestlands and meadows include 37 miles of groomed trails and 62 miles of back country trails. "Nordic skiing here brings pleasure and enjoyment to

• Trapp Family Cross Country Ski Center near the Lodge.

people," says Johannes. "It has been very rewarding. Vermont has been good to us and we are glad to return the favor."

A convert to cross country skiing was Maria von Trapp. "Thank God for Johannes's trails!" she exclaimed. She was also grateful that "Johannes did the impossible: he's taken the Lodge out of the red and put it on its own feet. What was difficult in the beginning turned out to be a real blessing. At our annual meeting, I expressed my admiration. I can imagine that my next book might be: 'How Not to Run a Lodge and Other Stories.'"

Johannes's effort to set the Lodge on firm financial ground evolved as a lifelong profession. He and Lynne settled near the Lodge. They raised their children, Kristina and Sam, with the same meadows, mountains and forests the earlier von Trapps cherished.

———

When asked about her favorite time at the Lodge, Maria automatically replied: "Christmas Eve." An immense evergreen tree, lit with wax candles, stood sentinel in the living room. Each Christmas Eve Maria presided over a gathering of lodgers, family, and friends. The candlelit pageantry included her storytelling and caroling *en masse*, with *Silent Night* as the finale. "Every Christmas Eve has its own magic," according to Maria.

On December 21, 1980, all was ready for the holiday when tragedy intervened. Deep in the night, fire swept through the wooden Lodge. A night watchman alerted guests who jumped from balconies and windows into 20 below temperatures. Guests at the adjacent Lower Lodge opened the doors to shaken evacuees, as the burning building nearby filled the night with horror.

Johannes was alerted. He raced to the site, seeing no one in evidence, unaware that guests were safely under shelter. He found his mother, in her nightgown and slippers. Her ninety-three year old secretary, Ethel Smalley, had awakened to a smoke-filled room in Maria's second floor apartment. She roused Maria and another friend, Emily Johnson. The three were saved by Lodge guest Jerry Lawrence who led them over a snowy balcony and down a slippery ladder. With Johannes, Maria watched their beloved home burn. "The big poplar tree at the entrance was on fire," Johannes remembered. "She asked me 'Is there something you can do about this?' I said 'No.' She just said 'All right.' She was wonderfully fatalistic. It was God's Will and God's Will be done."

Lorli recalled the fateful night: "Friends notified us of the fire. I saw the glow from Waitsfield. It looked like a harvest moon over the horizon. As I watched I felt a sob coming up right from my toes. I called Agathe to say 'It happened . . our father once dreamed the house was burning.'"

Stowe firefighters heroically attempted to quell the flames, but intense cold thwarted efforts. At dawn, only four chimneys remained surrounded by a ghostly swirl of steam and smoke. An explanation of the blaze was never pinpointed. Media spread the story world-wide; the von Trapps had lost their home a second time.

Observing the smoldering wreckage, Johannes told reporters: "We will rebuild." Ironically, the day after the fire a rug arrived in the

• **Remains of the Lodge the morning after.**

mail, crafted by Tibetan monks. The rug bore the family motto: "Nec aspera terrent", meaning "Let nothing difficult frighten you."

While limited hospitality was offered at the Austrian Tea Room and Lower Lodge, the momentous task of rebuilding spanned three years. Replacing the Trapp Family Lodge was a two-fold project: a 96-room hotel, and a time-share condominium village. Financing the construction, plus adhering to Vermont's strict development control laws, made the project a prolonged, complex undertaking.

In December 1983 the von Trapps welcomed the first guest to the rebuilt Lodge. It was a spectacular modern mountain hotel, with nostalgic features of the first inn. When Johannes toured his mother through the sprawling Lodge, she admitted: "I'm overwhelmed." Suite 300 was her new home.

A five-day Crowning Event Celebration commemorating another von Trapp triumph occurred in January 1984. Family and friends filled the Lodge, including missionary Maria from New Guinea, and Father Wasner from Salzburg. Banquets, interviews, and ABC-TV "Good Morning America" coverage culminated with a grand Austrian Ball. Maria's longtime friends, Mary Martin and Mrs. Bob Hope, were guests.

"I want to go home, but there is no home," remarked Maria after the fire. With her Vermont locus a gaping hole in the ground, she thought longingly of Austria. "I would go back," she said, "but I'd stay deep in the country where the old peasants live."

While a new Lodge was being constructed Maria lived in Stowe with Emily Johnson. Gone with the fire was a lifetime of family treasures and memorabilia. "I lost just plain everything, especially mementos of the old life," mourned Maria. The Captain's portrait, a focal point for guests in the Lodge dining room, was no more. Commissioned in Austria by Maria to surprise her husband, it was retrieved from Villa Trapp post-war.

"It is God's Will that we rebuild," Maria responded to the thousands who expressed their concern over the von Trapps' loss.

"It is one of the most beautiful parties I've been to," said Mary Martin. "I feel much honored to be a part of Maria's life." Maria's 79th birthday was observed during the gathering.

As Von Trapps and non-Trapps harmonized together, Maria glowed, misty-eyed. After each old favorite, Maria urged, "Sing some more!" They did.

Per Sørli presented Maria with a gift, a rare 1890 Norwegian ski; she was applauded. Her eloquence, charm and authority were intact as she graciously responded. Then Rupert quipped, "Per, Mother has *two* feet!"

Following the celebration Johannes was enthusiastic. "Now comes the fun part, running the place." Cross-country skiers glided past the Lodge, and vacationers filled the state-of-the art rooms. A new slogan was coined: *A Little of Austria, a Lot of Vermont.*

❦

Gradually Maria resumed her public life. With Rupert, she returned to Austria, appearing in a documentary shown by BBC. She was a celebrated personage when she appeared at the 1981 London revival of *The Sound of Music.*

- **Maria and Rupert at the Austrian Ball.**

- **middle photo, standing: Werner, Lorli, and Johannes.** **seated: Father Wasner, Maria, Rupert, Mother, and Mary Martin together for the *Crowning Event Celebration* officially opening the new Lodge**

- **Maria with the children, grandchildren, and spouses at the joyous opening of the new Lodge .**

Maria, escorted by grandson George, was an honored guest at White House state dinner for the President of Austria in 1984. President Reagan introduced her as "one of the best-loved of all Austrian-Americans. Perhaps more than any other American she has contributed to the deep friendship that our two nations enjoy." Maria chatted at length with the Reagans and the Bushes. She commented on a major gaffe during the Austrian president's visit. When "Edelweiss" from *The Sound of Music* was played, it was announced as Austria's national anthem!

In her final years, Maria was content to remain among her mountains. "The landscape of Vermont is so beautiful," she said. "I just look out at the Green Mountains and imagine the Austrian Alps behind them."

At 82, Maria was weary. Her formidable drive and determination had faded. "Mother seemed to flicker away like a candle," said Werner's wife Erika. When Maria's last illness was upon her, the family she led for so long gathered around their matriarch.

"We took watch over her, singing and praying," Werner said. "I asked her daughter Elisabeth to read from the fourteenth chapter of John: 'in my house there are many mansions...' Elisabeth, Lorli, and Hugh were singing 'To Thee the Holy Ghost We Now Pray' and just at that moment, Mother opened her eyes with an amazing gaze, and was gone." It was March 28, 1987.

The von Trapp family had lost its strong, creative leader. "It is the end of an era; she developed everything we have at the Lodge," said George, who worked there with his grandmother for years.

When news of Maria's passing spread through Stowe, she was remembered as a legend, a woman of faith, and a force as strong as a mountain when pursuing her convictions. To the world beyond she was fondly recalled as heroine of a classic play and film, the guiding force of one of history's beloved families. As Mary Martin said of her alter ego, "Maria didn't just climb that mountain. She helped everybody over it."

"My mother was an independent soul," Lorli remembered. "The song about her from *The Sound of Music* was so accurate. We teased her that it was the only truthful song in the whole movie!"

And how did Maria von Trapp reflect on her adventurous life? "I feel as if my life is like a story, a very, *very* beautiful story."

hapter 17

ife
t the
odge

Although the amenities of the Trapp Family Lodge lure visitors to the resort, the mystique of the family history is an ever present draw. Hallways, guest rooms and public spaces pay homage to the family past, with walls tastefully covered with framed family photographs: von Trapps on stage, working on the farm, building their house, and reveling in rural Vermont. Guests gaze at the historical panorama, commenting on the grit of their hosts-by-default.

While proud of von Trapp lore, Johannes stresses the Lodge's outdoor activities and outstanding natural setting. In 1986 he helped establish the Stowe Land Trust, dedicated to protecting the area's open spaces and rural character. This led to a conservation easement partnership with the Stowe Land Trust guaranteeing that 1500 acres of von Trapp land are preserved in natural forested condition. "This ensures that the land will remain scenically, ecologically and appropriately developed," explained Johannes.

The attraction of the Stowe area encouraged several von Trapp siblings to retire there. Rupert was first to return. After completing his thirty-two year medical career in Rhode Island and Massachusetts, he and his second wife Jan located in Stowe. Rosmarie was drawn

• **Celebrating 50 years in the USA:**
standing: **Rupert, Lorli, Maria, Johanna, Werner;**
seated: **Johannes and Rosmarie.**

back as well. She introduced sing-along sessions for Lodge guests, taught crafts and recorder lessons. In 1988 Maria returned to Vermont after finishing thirty years of missionary work in Papua New Guinea. She first lived in Waitsfield, and then moved to a chalet near the Lodge. Rupert, Maria and Rosmarie each enjoyed their proximity to the Lodge, and periodically blended into activities there.

• Fine dining is a hallmark of the Lodge. From casual to formal to family friendly, the von Trapps offer five restaurant settings, each with exceptional Green Mountain vistas.

• The Millennial Wing is an addition to the Lodge with guest rooms and facilities for large gatherings. Reunions, meetings, and family celebrations are held in the magnificent Mozart Room. It was the setting for the 90th birthday party of Maria (seen with pianist John Cassel.) Other meeting venues are named for composers Schubert and Strauss.

below: Afternoon tea accompanies mountain scenery seen from the living room, the library or the lounge.

"I'm just a kid from the woods," quips Sam von Trapp, seen above with sister Kristina von Trapp Frame. During elementary school, their first job at the Lodge was keeping cocoa stocked in the Outdoor Center. After college, they both taught skiing in various locales before becoming involved with the Lodge operation. Family History Tours were initiated; Kristina and Sam both meet and interact with guests. "My sister and I want to recognize and cherish our history, and connect with guests," says Sam. When Kristina is asked if she sings, her response is: "No better than anyone else!"

- top left: **Sam and Johannes head out from the Outdoor Center. To extend the season on the cross country ski trails, Sam introduced snow making.**

- center left: **Trapp Lager Marathon Ski Race.**

- left: **Family snowshoeing on the Trapp trails.**

Maria von Trapp wrote that first maple sugaring season on the farm was "one of our most lovely times in America. We never heard of maple syrup in Europe; now we were making it."

• left: **Martina glues labels on syrup cans; Agathe designed the labels.**

center and right: **Maria and Lorli prepare food for the family's "sugar on snow party" when the sugaring season concluded.**

Sugaring: Then and Now

• above and right:
The von Trapp sugar house is easily reached via snowshoes or cross-country skis. From late winter through early spring sap is collected and processed. Vermont produces 50% of the nation's pure maple syrup.

• above: **Originally this vintage structure was the Gale farmhouse;
then it was the home for Werner's family. It later became the
Tea Room-Gift Shop with a deck for dining, overlooking some of
Vermont's grandest views. It is now called The Kaffeehaus.**
Photo © Paul Rogers Photography

• above right: **Maria's favorite apple strudel, a Lodge tradition.**

• right: **Signage directing visitors to the miles of Lodge trails, used
ar-round by skiers, fitness enthusiasts, mountain bikers, and nature lovers.**

• below: **"My grandmother always said we can never have too many
wers," says Sam von Trapp. Tours of the spectacular gardens are offered.
ountiful vegetable gardens and farm fresh eggs provide Farm-to-Table
menu selections in Lodge dining rooms. Scotch Highlander beef cattle
have thrived at the Lodge since the 1960s. Guests are fascinated
y them; Maria called them "The most photographed cows in Vermont."**

Photo © Paul Rogers Photography

Von Trapp On Tap

- upper and middle left:
The brewery entrance and grand staircase greet guests with a mix of Austria and Vermont.

- right:
Sam, in Austrian garb, contrasts with the sleek stainless steel of the brewery tanks.

- lower right:
Four year-round beers — Golden Helles, Vienna Amber, Bohemian Pilsner, and Dunkel — plus five seasonal beers are in high demand in Vermont and other states.

- below:
Another slice of Austria in the hills of Vermont: the state-of-the-art brewery and bierhall opened in 2016.

Photo © Paul Rogers Photography

"When I visit Austria I am impressed by each town's local beer. Some small breweries date back to the 1400s. Their beers are unique, complex lagers unavailable here. For decades I dreamed of brewing craft beers in Vermont. We have our own pure spring water, perfect for brewing. In 2010 we opened our first humble brewery in bakery space. The response to our beer was tremendous. There is nothing more Austrian than a bierhall!", says Johannes, pictured above.

- upper left:
  Looking down on a portion of the Bierhall Restaurant.

- left:
  A glass of the award-winning Von Trapp Lager.

• left:
The Outdoor Center on a beautiful fall day. Guests will find selections of outdoor equipment to rent for every season.

• right:
Lodge life includes wagon rides in the spring, summer or fall. A relaxing option for taking in the incredible scenery.

• **A panoramic view of the Lodge grounds.**

• The Lodge on a cold, starry night. On New Years Eve there is a customary ringing of the bell above the entrance, and a display of fireworks. The Lodge's Christmas Eve event includes Johannes and Lynne; Kristina and husband Walter Frame with their daughters; and Sam and wife Becky with their two sons.

• below: Musical icons: Rosmarie and resident pianist John Cassel play a Christmas duet. The affable John entertained at the Lodge for thirty years.

• **Captain Georg von Trapp**
1880-1947

Chapter 18

The Von Trapps: A Lasting Legacy

Despite the renown of the *Trapp Family Singers*, Captain von Trapp's children never felt that their father was adequately honored for his exemplary life. His reputation as an Austrian navy hero, his gallantry in opposing Nazism, and his efforts in saving lives through the Austrian Relief were known, but the father figure they knew was somehow overshadowed by the family fame. In 1997, fifty years after his death, the Captain was finally commemorated.

Cadets at Austria's Military Academy, the Theresianum, voted Georg von Trapp as the patron and hero of their 1997 graduating class. A visit by Maria von Trapp and her nephew Tobi to the Theresianum transpired.

- **After placing a wreath on the Captain's grave, the cadets saluted their class role model as the von Trapp children looked on.**

"The welcome we received was overwhelming," said Maria. "We were so touched that these young cadets, so many years since World War I, chose our father as their hero. I invited them to come to Trapp Family Lodge. Immediately the commandant said, "Yes we will come in 1997, the year of this classes' graduation."

At the command of the Austrian defense minister, with clearance by the United States, 89 cadets arrived at the Lodge on the morning of July 11, 1997. In the early dawn Maria and Johannes welcomed the Austrians who came to honor their family's patriarch.

• **The Theresianum Military Class of 1997 with the Captain's children.**
from left: **Rosmarie, Lorli, Werner, Agathe, Maria, and Johannes. The Captain was ahead of his time in parenting.**
He was a stay-at-home father, a house-husband, a child-centered parent, and the head of a blended family.
Photo © David Wade

In fatigues and combat boots the cadets joined Johannes on a six mile hike over the mountain terrain known by the Captain in the 1940s. Meanwhile, three generations of von Trapp descendants assembled at the Lodge. "Having the family together is important, especially for the third and fourth generations," noted Johannes. The Captain's living children were present: Agathe, Maria, Werner, Rosmarie, Lorli, and Johannes. A Sunday field Mass was celebrated, in view of the Captain's burial site. Schubert's *German Mass* was sung, accompanied by the Vermont

Mozart Festival Orchestra. Once more the Captain's children rose to sing, with the cadets nearby, and the Green Mountains surrounding them all.

The event also had political significance. Austrian Consul General Dr. Walter Greinert acknowledged that the cadets' tribute affirmed the righteous decision of the Captain to lead his family out of their Nazi-occupied homeland nearly sixty years earlier. Cadet Rainer Winter likened the Captain's life to the Academy's motto: *Good Officers and Righteous Men*. "His was a remarkable life to inspire all of us," said Cadet Winter,

as his comrades placed a commemorative wreath on the Captai grave. "He cared for his men, and they rewarded him with their trust. Georg von Trapp's decision to leave Austria rather than serve in the armed forces of Adolf Hitle was a difficult one. We think he made the right decision."

Dr. Greinert mentioned that celebrating the Captain was a mea of healing the dark memory of th Nazi regime. "I am here as a repre sentative of a new Austria in a ne Europe," he stated. We are a new generation now, putting behind u some of the troubles of the past."

Of the three day celebration of her father, Maria simply said "It is like a dream. We are thrilled at the thought that Austria has not forgotten our father." ~

• The family cemetery. "From there the Captain is still running the ship," said Maria von Trapp.

BACK TO BROADWAY

On March 12, 1998 the von Trapps were in New York for opening night of the Broadway revival of *The Sound of Music*. It was also Agathe's 85th birthday, and sixty years since the Nazis invaded Austria. Agathe, Maria, Rosmarie, and Johannes were properly lionized. They seemed to enjoy the media blitz thoroughly, graciously cooperating like the pros they were. At a post-premiere celebration at Tavern on the Green, the von Trapps mingled with the cast of *The Sound of Music*. The play continued through a teen month run.

In December the von Trapps were back in New York. The State of Salzburg honored the remaining family members and their seven movie counterparts. There hadn't yet been a meeting of the two "families." They spied each other from afar. Warm, outgoing Maria sauntered over to break the ice. Her broad smile embraced the now grown up actors. "Now you are family!" she announced. "I had an overwhelming sense of belonging," recalled Charmian Carr, Liesl in the film. There was applause when Vice Governor Dr. Gasteiger extolled the von Trapps' impact on Salzburg. He then presented the *Golden Decoration of Honor* to Agathe, Maria, Werner, Rosmarie, Lorli, and Johannes. *The Mozart Medal* was then awarded to each of the movie von Trapps: Charmian Carr, Nicholas Hammond, Heather Menzies, Duane Chase, Angela Cartwright, Debbie Turner, and Kym Karath. Then came an unexpected highlight of the evening. The *Trapp Family Singers* stood to sing. One more time it was *Silent Night, Holy Night* ... first in German, then in English. "There was something godlike in their combined voices, their intricate harmonies ..." said Charmian Carr of the mesmerizing performance. The singing continued. Both versions of the von Trapp "children" sang *Edelweiss* together. The audience joined in.

Agathe von Trapp spoke for her family: "We never expected to be honored for anything. Because of *The Sound of Music* our name reached every nation on earth. It is good to know that our homeland has not forgotten us. Is it not easy to see the hand of God in all this?"

Photo © Anita & Steve Shevett   ❀ **185**

ELISABETH

Growing up in Werner and Erika von Trapp's household meant immersion in music. The children were accustomed to a home filled with a piano, guitars, a harp, and motley baroque instruments. They went to sleep with the sounds of Vivaldi, Mozart, and Bach wafting up the stairs. Werner's voice and guitar was a mellow accompaniment to their lives. As a busy dairy farmer, it seemed he paused only for church and music.

"Just one more song," Maria von Trapp urged when the family gathered at the Lodge. "We children didn't mind," Elisabeth remembers. "None of us wanted to go to bed!" Those occasions exposed Elisabeth to the intricate harmonies of her aunts and uncles. Visiting her maternal grandmother in Austria further awakened her passion for guitar and singing. Back home in Vermont, she sang in town halls, at weddings and in churches. Like many of her cousins, Elisabeth also worked for her grandmother at the Tea Room and Gift Shop. Eventually Elisabeth performed regularly for Lodge guests, and played Maria in a production of *The Sound of Music*.

Elisabeth studied music in college, taught a year, and married attorney Ed Hall. Her career as a singer steadily evolved as she toured nationally and internationally. "I remember being so excited when I told my parents I had signed for 100 concerts," Elisabeth recalls. Then remembering his own days on the road, Werner quipped, "You poor thing!" Her husband and parents were wholeheartedly supportive. Elisabeth's career unfolded to include recordings, Christmas tours with *The Empire Brass*, and solo concerts. Elisabeth's voice has been called "breathtaking with lyrics tender and romantic." Her repertoire is an eclectic mix of music: folk, classical, and pop. Elisabeth describes it as "Bach to Broadway, Schubert to Sting, and everything in-between." There is always an onstage nod to songs from *The Sound of Music*, and a tribute to her father's family. She explains "Music is something I need to do to stay alive. It lifts my spirit, and I believe it does for the audience."
www.elisabethvontrapp.com

third generation of Werner's
family lit up the world's theater
marquees as *The Von Trapp Children*.
His grandchildren, Sofia, Amanda,
Melanie, and Justin, offspring of
Stefan and Annie, lived in Montana.
During summer visits Werner
taught them Austrian folk songs.
"He and Oma sat through our variety
shows around the kitchen table,"
says Amanda.

One summer Werner's health
precluded a visit. The grandchildren
recorded some songs, to cheer him.
Then pianist George Winston discovered the siblings, inviting them
to sing during his concerts through
Montana. *The Von Trapp Children*
were born as a singing group.

Wearing Austrian outfits, the kids
evoked fond images of *The Sound of
Music*. Their mother explained "The
door was opened because of their
name." But they still had to prove
themselves as performers. They did.
Justin, Melanie, Sofia, and Amanda
spent 2001-2016 as professional
singers. Their pleasing personalities
and ever-expanding vocal ranges
made them concerts hits. They sang
everywhere from Carnegie Hall
to the Sydney Opera House. The
"Oprah" show, celebrating the 45th
anniversary of *The Sound of Music*,
asked the kids to sing *Edelweiss*
with the movie von Trapps. When

the show aired, another raft of
offers arrived. The kids' career
mirrored that of their singing
ancestors, this time with 21st century
hype. On most tours the Von Trapps
traveled with their parents, and they
were home schooled. "Such enforced
togetherness is a blessing not a
chore," replied Sophia. Each sibling
pursued individual passions: soccer,
baseball, hiking, and "just being kids."

A new era began when *The Von
Trapps* (their newly updated name)
performed with Thomas Lauderdale's
eclectic band, *Pink Martini*. They
collaborated on the album *Dream

a Little Dream* and morphed into
a modern Indie band. In 2016
The Von Trapps announced: "After
years of performing and carrying
on our family tradition, we have
chosen to close this chapter in
our lives to pursue individual
dreams and interests."

Chapter 19

The Captain's Children ... "We Grew Up!"

...uests visiting the Lodge ...en now expect us to still ...ok like children!"
— Lorli von Trapp Campbell

...group of brothers and ...ters is something so ...ecious. They work ...gether and learn from ...ildhood to watch out ...r each other and to share."
— Maria von Trapp

...rapp Family Lodge is ...till the gathering place ...or special occasions. ...eated: Agathe and Maria ...anding: Rosmarie, Johannes, ...nd Lorli.

RUPERT

Rupert perhaps lived the most independent life of all his brothers and sisters. But following his retirement from medicine he re-entered the family orbit in Stowe, where several of his children and some of his siblings lived nearby. During retirement, music returned to Rupert's life, his passion after medicine. He collaborated with his second wife Jan on *The Pied Piper's Repertoire*, a series of books for recorder players. Jan, a cellist and teacher, brought continuous music to their home with frequent rehearsals and lessons. "I seem to be informally a resident coach-critic," Rupert said. "I have come full circle, hearing chamber music in my home, and still loving it!" Of his own siblings, Rupert said "We're close, but not as close as the touring days. We are poor letter writers! And *The Sound of Music* hasn't changed us one bit." Regular visits to Austria re-connected Rupert with his roots and relatives there, until his death at 80 in 1992.

AGATHE

Agathe assisted Mary Lou Kane in the operation of Sacred Heart Kindergarten near Baltimore until retiring in 1993. With Mary Lou, Agathe traveled widely. She made regular trips to Stowe, and returns to Austria. A dedicated historian,

Photo © Molly Peters

she researched her von Trapp forebears, compiling a genealogy for her relatives. After years of living quietly and eschewing notoriety, Agathe wrote her autobiography: *Memories Before and After The Sound of Music* (Harper Collins, 2003). She was 90 when the book was published. Agathe relished the resulting flurry of interviews, book promotions, and signings. Her book was adapted as a European-made film: *A Life of Music*. Agathe continued to paint, sketch, write, play guitar and piano, and travel well into her eighties and nineties. She sang with Johannes and Maria before a large Salzburg audience. She also joined her great nieces and nephew, the *Von Trapp Children*, in a Christmas concert, playing a guitar and singing. Agathe passed in 2010 at the age of 97. Of her life she remarked, "I would not have wanted to do anything else. We sang so well together; it was a wonderful feeling."

MARIA

Maria's vibrant presence, ready laughter, and love of people enhanced life at the Lodge during the twenty years she lived in a cozy home nearby. She was periodically joined there by her adopted son Kikuli. After completing several

college degrees, Kikuli moved to Vermont to teach mathematics. He and Werner encouraged Maria to collect, translate, and publish songs she sang with her siblings during their youth in Austria. The result was *My Favorite Songs: Maria von Trapp's Childhood Folk Songs* (Veritas Press). "I want people to sing," Maria explained, "and Austrian melodies are very easy to sing." Maria continued to travel, give interviews, speak publicly, and play accordion enthusiastically into her nineties. She welcomed visiting family and friends to the Lodge, endearing herself to everyone. In 2014, seven months short of her 100th birthday, Maria died at home, with Kikuli by her side. She was the last of the seven von Trapp children who had made musical history. "If the world sang together, there could be no war," Maria declared. "Music is like food; we need it regularly."

WERNER

Werner and Erika retired from farming in 1979, moving to a country home nearby. Their dairy farm was continued by son Martin and his family. Werner said of his retirement: "There is never a dull moment in my life and not enough time to do the things I could or would do." He and Erika traveled, especially to Austria. Many of their

Photo © David Wade

six children and grandchildren lived nearby, making frequent visits. Gardens surrounded Werner and Erika's home, and sheep grazed on their acreage. Werner was by nature a humble, quiet man, and he said "I am glad I'm thirty miles from Stowe and not drawn into it" — meaning the epicenter of von Trapp fame. Instead, Werner and Erika were active in *The Valley Friendly Spinners' Guild*. Werner wove rugs, crocheted, and was busy with handicrafts. His agricultural tradition continues with his son Tobi's *Von Trapp Greenhouse*, and his grandsons' production of artisan cheese on the family farm. Werner died at home in 2007, at the age of 91. His last days were filled, as Erika said, "with a row of visits before his final goodbye, when the Lord took him to Himself with mercy, caring and love."

HEDWIG

"I wouldn't want any other life," said Hedwig of her concert career. "I think there is nothing so wonderful as knowing and appreciating good music." Her sister Agathe observed: "Hedwig had a heart for young people." She taught in Hawaii during the 1960s, a climate favorable to her asthmatic condition. A student recalled that "Miss Trapp was the biggest influence of my life. She is the reason I've made music most of my life. She taught

four and six-part harmonies to Masses, along with crafts,

arpentry, cooking and sewing." After working stints at the Trapp family Lodge, Hedwig taught at a Tyrolean village school in the Austrian Alps. In 1972 Hedwig was back at her birthplace in Zell am See. She lived peacefully with her Tante Joan Whitehead until an asthma attack ended her life at age 55. Following her burial in the family cemetery at the Trapp Family Lodge, Werner offered Hedwig's spinning wheel to Carol Collins, a family friend. "This led me to my decades of wool and spinning business," said Carol. No doubt Hedwig, the inveterate craftsperson, would be proud.

JOHANNA

Until her marriage, Johanna was lead soprano of the *Trapp Family Singers*. Her musicality extended to guitar, recorder, piano and clarinet.

Photo © David Wade

Her artistic versatility matched her musical skills: watercolor, sculpting, illuminations, calligraphy, and ceramics. As Professor Ernst Winter's wife, and mother of seven, Johanna was absorbed in homemaking. The Winters engaged in organic farming and a back-to-the-earth lifestyle on their rural New York state acreage. In 1961 Ernst became head of a research institute in Salzburg. The family returned to Johanna's homeland. They next moved to Vienna, where Ernst headed the Austrian Diplomatic Academy. The Winters became caretakers of Schloss Eichbüchl, a castle where large student groups gathered for seminars. With her children's help, Johanna supplied meals and hospitality for participants. Following that era, and the marriages of her children, Johanna spent time in America. A stroke slowed her, but not her artistic endeavors. She joined Ernst, who worked for the United Nations, on business travels, and reunions with their children around the globe. While the couple lived in Vienna, Johanna died peacefully in 1994 at the age of 75.

MARTINA

"Martina was everyone's favorite," said Rupert of his sister, who died in childbirth in 1951. With the

family on tour in California, Rupert and Rosmarie were the only siblings present when Martina and her child were buried near the Captain. "She is still sorely missed," Rupert said years later. Their second mother shared Rupert's sentiments. "When I was quite sick," Maria wrote, "she had always taken care of me, spent weeks with me in the hospital, and nursed me back to health; always patient, always cheerful, full of little surprises...a bouquet of wild flowers or a hand-painted card...in art she was a master."

ROSMARIE

"Mother and I had a special connection. I was her first-born and resembled her," said Rosmarie. Like her mother, she shared an affinity for helping others and traveling the world. Rosmarie's peripatetic youth followed her all her life, even after settling in Stowe in the 1990s. She traveled widely, speaking to audiences about her life, faith, and family.

She adapted effortlessly to all age groups and settings. Rosmarie shared her belief that mistakes are overcome with God's faithfulness. She delighted groups with singalongs and played guitar and recorder during performances. In her seventies Rosmarie volunteered at *Biblical Tamar Archeological Park*, south of Israel's Dead Sea. "History became real to me," she said, "seeing unearthed artifacts from King Solomon's era." At home, Rosmarie remained an enthused craftsperson, meeting regularly with the *Valley Friendly Spinners Guild*. "We loved her creativity and giving nature," said a fellow spinner. Rosmarie's beautifully wrought caps, coverlets, socks and slippers (made with wool she carded and spun herself) are part of her loving legacy. She was the last of the seven von Trapp sisters when she died in 2022 at age 93. Beloved by family, friends, and the Stowe community, her February 8th birthday is now observed at the Trapp Family Lodge as *"Rosmarie's Kindness Day."*

LORLI

Lorli and Hugh Campbell settled in their mountain chalet home near

Photo © David Wade

Waitsfield in 1975. The property had an artesian well, a pond, and ample garden space. "Lorli, the beauty of our family, takes great interest in plants and people," said Rupert. "She is the most hospitable person I know." Lorli's gracious hospitality was legendary, especially at Christmas time when a sixteen-foot candlelit tree was the focal point of the Campbell home. Lorli's lyrical speaking voice launched easily into her memories of performing Christmas concerts with her family and growing up in Vermont. When asked as an adult to join other singing groups, she demurred. *"I can't"*, she admitted. "It was just too unique, singing with my family." Lorli understood the mass appeal of *The Sound of Music*. "People need hope and our story shows that trust in God is honored." This is the legacy that Lorli shared with her ever-growing family, right up to her death in 2021 at the age of 90.

JOHANNES

The young boy who explored the forests and fields of the von Trapp farm has spent a near-lifetime dedicated to the nurture of his family home place. Johannes played a pivotal role in Stowe's hospitality industry and winter sports culture, seamlessly blending them with Vermont's environment. He is also the forefather of North America's first commercial cross-country ski touring center. Trapps' operation is still unrivaled in North America. "My father has an eye for aesthetics,"

says Sam. "He also has vision; his imprint is evident everywhere at the Lodge and its environs." Of the family influence that still pervades the Lodge in the 21st century Johannes says, "We were about good taste, culture and

wonderful European standards. My brothers and sisters were creative, painting pictures, making jewelry, and so on. I wasn't, so I put my creativity into the Lodge." Sam and Kristina have shouldered responsibilities, but Johannes remains very involved. The younger of the von Trapp children has come full circle. He is patriarch of three generations of von Trapps who live and work on the land chosen by Georg and Maria when they first saw it decades ago. Johannes still extends this invitation: *"We invite you to share the grandeur of this place, once our home, now the Trapp Family Lodge."*   ~

Conductor Robert Shaw considered the von Trapps "The greatest choral group in the history of recorded sound." Their recordings have been reissued continuously through the years. At this writing the most definitive, remastered collections are the compact disc sets, **One Voice** and **Journey,** on the Jasmine label.

RCA VICTOR

Recorded 12/16/38: Innsbruck, ich muss dich lassen; Landsknechständchen (***Soldier's Serenade***); Es ist ein Ros Entsprungren (***Lo, How a Rose e're Blooming***); Frienslieb du hast mich gefangen (***My Love, You Have Bewitched Me***); Tanzen und Springen (***Dancing and Skipping***)

Recorded 12/17/38: Zu Bethlehem Geboren (***In Bethlehem Born***); Wohlauf ihr lieben Gäste (***Now Then, Dear Guests***); Die Martigans (***St. Martin's Goose***); Ein Hennlein Weiss (***A Little White Hen***); Mein eingis A (***My Own A***); Il Bianco e dolce Cigno (***The Sweet White Swan***)

Recorded 12/21/38: Wach Auf, Wach Auf (***Awake, Awake***); Der Mond is Aufgegangen (***The Moon Has Risen***); Come Heavy Sleep; Andreas Hofer's Abschied von Leben (***Farewell to Life***); In einem kuhlen Grunde (***In a Cool Dale***); Bist einmel kommen (***Once Thou Camest to Redeem Us***)

Recorded 12/22/38: Es Wird scho glei dumpa (***It's Getting Dark***); Der Spate Abend (***Late One Evening***); Lavanthal, Lavanthal (***Valley of Lavant***); Maria durch ein Dornwald ging (***In the Thorny Woods***)

Recorded 10/16/39: An all Bach recording session. O Haupt Voll Blut und Wunden (***Oh Head All Scarred and Bleeding***); Wie Schön Leuchet der Morgenstern; Jesu Meine Freude

Recorded 10/17/39: More Bach recordings: Von Himmel Hoch (***From Heaven High***); Nun Danket Alle Gott; Lobt Gott ihr Christen Allzugleich; Wer Nur den Lieben Gott Lässt Walten

Recorded 10/18/39: Wachet Auf Ruft uns Die Stimme; Lobe Den Herren; Dir, Dir Jehova; Netherlands Dances for Recorders: Rondo, Pavane, Intrade, Sarabande, Gigue

Recorded 02/05/40: An all Brahms recording session. Guten Abend, Gut Nacht; Waldesnacht; In Stiller Nacht; Lullaby

Recorded 02/20/40: Selections from Palestrina's Missa Brevis including Kyrie, Gloria, Agnus Dei

Recorded 02/21/40: Stille Nacht (***Silent Night***), **selections from Missa Brevis:** Gloria, Part 2, Credo, Part 1, Credo, Conclusion, Sanctus, Benedictus, Away in a Manger; Eriskay Love Lilt; Kindersegen (***Child's Blessing***)

Recorded 06/26/41: (Recorded at the Academy of Music in Philadelphia) Midwinter; God Rest You Merry, Gentlemen; Cradle Song; In Dulce Jubilo

CONCERT HALL SERIES

The CONCERT HALL SOCIETY label recorded the von Trapps' first long-playing record albums in 1950. Personnel: *Maria Augusta Trapp, Father Wasner, Agathe, Maria, Werner, Hedwig, Martina, Lorli, and Johannes.*

At Home With The Trapp Family Singers

Released in 1950: Meerstern, ich Dich grüsse; The Children's Blessing; Jesu, Joy of Man's Desiring; Fahren wir froh im Nachen; Ein Hennlein Weiss; The Soldiers Serenade; The Silver Swan; Pastorale (instrumental); Siliciana and Allegro (instrumental); Austrian Folk Dance (instrumental); Und Wan I Geh; Vom Zillertal Aussa; Echo Yodel; Old Black Joe; Riquiran; Evening Prayer from Hänsel & Gretel

Sacred Music Around the Church Year

A musical recording of the liturgical year from Advent through Pentecost: Sanctus and Benedictus; Maria durch ein Dornwald ging; Psallite Unigenito; Jesu Redemptor Omnium; Resonet in Laudibus; O Bone Jesu; Jesu, Salvator Mundi; O Salutaris Hostia; Wer Leucht' uns denn bei der finsteren Nacht?; Crux Fidelis; Tenebrae Factae Sunt; Surrexit Pastor Bonus; Regina Coeli, Laetare; To Thee Holy Ghost We Now Pray; O Maria Diana Stella; Salve Regina

THE MUSICAL GENIUS OF FRANZ WASNER

• **Pope John Paul II greets Father Wasner**

Father Wasner spent fifteen years as director of "Anima", the German House of Theological Studies in Rome before his retirement in 1982. He then returned to Salzburg, becoming a canon of the Cathedral. Composing and playing music filled Father Wasner's life until his death in 1992 at the age of 86. Linda Radtke, choral music performer, paid tribute to the von Trapps' repertoire, all chosen, arranged and conducted by Father Wasner ..."What I hear on Trapp Family recordings is an amazing purity, a unison that seems effortless. That apparent ease was the result of tireless work, rehearsals, and the genius of Franz Wasner. Without question, their repertoire advanced choral music in this country. Before the revival of Early Music, the Trapps brought Palestrina and Praetorius to concert halls across America. Long before the folk music revival, Father Wasner arranged cowboy songs, Maori chants, and Austrian yodels, expertly jumbled together in their concerts. Their Christmas albums thrill me the most. It's a commitment to the music, a joy in telling the story — all hallmarks of true artistry. These recordings helped make them stars. The joy and beauty of their voices still come through, bright and clear."

Christmas With The Trapp Family Singers

Recorded in 1951, selections included: Es ist ein Ros entsprungen; Hirten, wachet auf!; Zu Bethlehem Gebohren; Deck the Hall; A la Nanita Nana; Il est né, le divin infant; La canzone di Natale; Es hat sich heut' eröffnet; Jesus, Jesus, Rest Your Head; Shepherds Come a-Running; Lobt-Gott, ihr Christen alle gleich; Es wird scho glei dumpa; Nu är det Jul igen; Ihr Kinderlein, kommet; Der Scheibendudler; Carol of the Drum; Deine Wangelen; Stille Nacht

Christmas With The Trapp Family Singers Vol. 2

Recorded in 1953, included singers and instrumentalists Charlene & Harold Peterson. Selections included: Angelus Ad Pastores In Nativitate Domini; Puer Natus Est Nobis; Beata Viscera; Pastorale (Recorders); Quem Pastores Laudavere; Senex Puerum Portabat; Ave Maria; I Sing of a Maiden; El Rorro; The Christmas Nightingale; Bring Your Torches; Jeanette, Isabella; Angels We Have Heard On High; Bethlehem; The Christmas Rose; Quittez, Pasteurs; Pastores a Belen; From Heaven On High

Sad I Am Without Thee

Recorded in 1953, also included the Petersons. Selections included: Alt Niederlandische Tanze (Recorders); Innsbruck, ich muss dich lassen; Kuckkuck hat sich zu tod gefall'n; Trio Sonata for Recorders (Telemann); In einem kuhlen grunde; Muss i' denn; Jagerleid; The Farmer's Boy; Every Year Brings Something New; The Lone Prairie; Trio (Instrumental by Hook); An Eriskay Love Lilt; Early One Morning

An Evening of Folk Songs With The Trapp Family Singers

Recorded in 1953, also included the Petersons. Selections included: S'Dirndl is' Wunderschön; Spinning Song; Der Grü; Die Hoch Alma; Andreas Hofer's Abcshied vom Leben; Que Lejos Estoy, Chilecito; Varmlandvisan; Luar Do Sertao; Sur la route de Dijon; J'entends le Moulin; La haut sur ces Montagnes; Easter Eggs

Farewell Concert

Recorded in 1956, personnel included: Peter LaManna, Annette Brophy, Alvaro Villa and Barbara Stechow. Selections included: Sing We Chant It; Il Bianco e Dolce Cigno; Song of Parting; Dein Herzlein Mild; In Stiller Nacht; Tota Pulchra es Maria; Peters Bruennerle Pokare kare ana; Waltzing Matilda; Hawaiian Wedding Song; Aloha Oe (Hawaiian Wedding Song is a duet with Annette Brophy and Father Wasner).

Chronology

1880	Georg Johannes von Trapp born
1891	Agathe Whitehead born
1905	Maria Augusta Kutschera born
1905	Franz Wasner born
1911	January: Marriage of Georg von Trapp & Agathe Whitehead November: Rupert born
1913	Agathe born
1914	Maria born
1915	Werner born
1917	Hedwig born
1919	Johanna born
1921	Martina born
1922	Agathe Whitehead von Trapp dies
1925	Trapp family moves to Salzburg
1926	Maria Kutschera a novice at Nonnberg Abbey
1927	Maria a governess at Trapp home; marriage of Georg & Maria
1929	Rosmarie born
1931	Eleonore born
1935-37	Formation of Trapp Family Choir and early concert tours
1938	Austria annexed by Germany; Trapp family leaves Salzburg; first American concert tour
1939	Johannes born; tours of Europe & United States
1942	Trapp Family buys Stowe, Vermont farm
1943	Rupert and Werner enter U.S. Army
1944	First season of Trapp Family Music Camp
1945	End of WWII; safe return of Rupert & Werner
1947	Establishment of Trapp Family Austrian Relief; death of Georg von Trapp

1948	Family members become American citizens; Werner married; Johanna married
1949	"The Story of the Trapp Family Singers" published; marriage of Martina
1950	Trapp Family Singers tour South America
1951	Death of Martina
1954	Eleonore married
1955	Australia-New Zealand concert tour
1956	Final concert performances; Music Camp disbands; German film "Die Trapp Familie" released
1959	"The Sound of Music" debuts on Broadway
1965	"The Sound of Music" released as a movie
1969	Johannes married; cross-country skiing is pioneered at the Trapp Family Lodge
1972	Death of Hedwig
1980	Trapp Family Lodge destroyed by fire; rebuilt Lodge opened in 1983
1987	Death of Maria Augusta von Trapp
1992	Death of Rupert
1992	Death of Franz Wasner
1994	Death of Johanna
2007	Death of Werner
2010	Death of Agathe
2014	Death of Maria
2016	Establishment of new Bierhall Restaurant
2021	Death of Lorli
2022	Death of Rosmarie

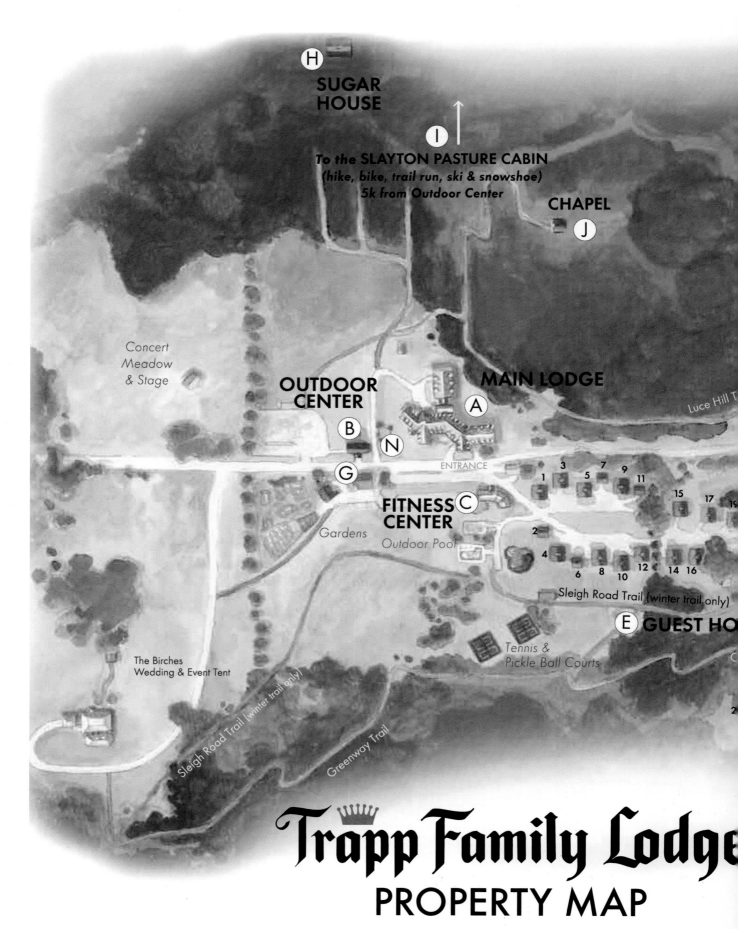

H
SUGAR
HOUSE

I

To the SLAYTON PASTURE CABIN
(hike, bike, trail run, ski & snowshoe)
5k from Outdoor Center

CHAPEL
J

*Concert
Meadow
& Stage*

OUTDOOR
CENTER
B

MAIN LODGE
A

Luce Hill T...

N

ENTRANCE

G

3   7   9
1   5   11
15   17   19

FITNESS
CENTER **C**

Gardens

Outdoor Pool

2

4

6   8   10   12   14   16

Sleigh Road Trail *(winter trail only)*

E ### GUEST HO...

*The Birches
Wedding & Event Tent*

*Tennis &
Pickle Ball Courts*

Sleigh Road Trail (winter trail only)

Greenway Trail

Trapp Family Lodge
PROPERTY MAP

MAP KEY

A MAIN LODGE
- Main Dining Room
- Gift Shops
- Meeting Spaces
- Real Estate Office
- Lounge

B OUTDOOR CENTER
- Rent bikes, helmets and other summer gear
- Rent skis, boots, poles, snowshoes in the winter
- Sign up for tours

C FITNESS CENTER
- Exercise Classes
- Hot Tub & Pool
- Sauna
- Climbing Wall
- Massage Treatments
- Yoga
- Mountain Kids Club
- Tennis/Pickle Ball Courts

D KAFFEEHAUS

E GUEST HOUSES

F THE VILLAS

G GREENHOUSE

H SUGARHOUSE

I THE CABIN

J CHAPEL

K LAUNDRY

L BIERHALL

M DISC GOLF

N FAMILY CEMETERY

F THE VILLAS

D KAFFEEHAUS

K LAUNDRY

Luce Hill Road

Town of Stowe
4.5 miles

M DISC GOLF

Lager Lane Trail

Sleigh Road Trail
(winter trail only)

L

BIERHALL RESTAURANT & BREWERY

WILLIAM ANDERSON is an award-winning historian, author, and educator. He has written 30 books of history, biography and travel, and published over 100 articles in national and international magazines.

For children he has written *V is for Von Trapp:
A Musical Family Alphabet*
(Sleeping Bear Press) and other perennial favorites.
His home is in Michigan.

www.williamandersonbooks.com